MATH TREK

MATH TREK

Adventures in the MathZone

· ·

IVARS PETERSON

and

NANCY HENDERSON

JOSSEY-BASS
A Wiley Imprint
www.josseybass.com

Credits

page 6: Courtesy of Nicholas R.Cozzarelli, University of California, Berkeley; page 18: Photograph of Carroll courtesy of Gernsheim Collection, Harry Ransom Humanities Research Center, The University of Texas at Austin; page 27: Photo courtesy of Heleman Ferguson; page 35: Boyer-Viollet; page 44: Photograph of Mandelbrot courtesy of IBM Research; pages 54 and 61: Courtesy of Sellner Manufacturing Co., Faribault, Minnesota; page 80: Hulton Getty/Liason Agency; illustrations on pages 1, 7, 9, 11, 12, 14, 19–23, 24 (bottom), 26, 29, 39, 53, 63–65, 73, 81, 83, 88, 91, and 99; © 1999 Jessica Wolk-Stanley.

Published simultaneously in Canada
Design and production by Navta Associates, Inc.

Published by Jossey-Bass
A Wiley Imprint
989 Market Street, San Francisco, CA 94103-1741   www.josseybass.com

Jossey-Bass books and products are available through most bookstores. To contact Jossey-Bass directly call our Customer Care Department within the U.S. at 800-956-7739, outside the U.S. at 317-572-3986, or fax 317-572-4002.

Jossey-Bass also publishes its books in a variety of electronic formats. Some content that appears in print may not be available in electronic books.

Library of Congress Cataloging-in-Publication Data

Peterson, Ivars.
     Math trek : adventures in the MathZone/Ivars Peterson and Nancy
Henderson.
          p.   cm.
     Includes bibliographical references and index.
     Summary: Explores various mathematical concepts—such as knots, fractals, secret codes, and chaos theory—and relates them to everyday life.
     ISBN 0-471-31570-2
     1. Mathematical recreations—Juvenile literature.
     [1. Mathematical recreations.]   I. Henderson, Nancy
     II. Title.
QA95.P435   1999   99-25900
793.7'4—dc21

Printed in the United States of America
FIRST EDITION
PB Printing   10 9 8 7 6 5

Contents..........................

Preface..

What do mathematicians really do? They start with the math that you study in school. They use numbers, arithmetic, geometry, algebra, and calculus. Then mathematicians also wander far afield. They tackle tricky logic problems, explore mind-boggling mental mysteries, and investigate hidden patterns in the universe. Along the way, they often amuse themselves with mathematical puzzles and games.

Whether math is your best or worst subject in school, we think you will enjoy visiting the MathZone and doing some of the things that mathematicians do.

Somewhere along the Interstate, where the highway is 19 lanes wide, stands a sign that says, "MathZone: Exit 11101101." The exit ramp is no simple cloverleaf; it winds around and crosses back over the highway, then twists under itself in a tangled roadway that ends up at a spiral-shaped parking lot.

From parking space 12358, a fractal-lined footpath leads to the MathZone amusement park. Go inside and climb the creaky Fun House stairs, scramble your senses on the Tilt-A-Whirl, bounce around like a pinball, or try your luck on the Boredwalk.

Whether you make the trek on your own, or with a friend, a parent, or a teacher, each MathZone adventure will take you deeper into the amazing world of modern mathematics. If you get stuck along the way, go to the back of the book to find the answers.

MATH TREK

Do Knot Enter

You are bicycling along a straight, smooth path. Suddenly the path bends sharply. It leads you under a bridge then loops back over itself, crossing the bridge and bending some more. It twists under and over itself again and finally brings you to a tall yellow brick wall.

As you follow the path along the wall, you begin to hear bells dinging, motors whirring, and children laughing. At the end of the path, you come to a massive gate made of knotty pinewood, marked with a glaring neon sign.

The word *Knot* is flashing on and off. You can't see through the gate, but when you look up, you observe the top of a Ferris wheel. You hear people cheering and chattering. Raucous music blares in the background. To the right, kids are spinning around on a crazy-looking flying saucer. To the left, a roller coaster looms above the wall.

MathZone? It looks more like an amusement park than a study hall!

Your eyes turn to five tangled loops of rope hanging from hooks on the gate. To the right of the gate is an empty ticket window with a sign that says, "Tickets Knot Required."

Puzzled, you lock your bike to a lamp-post, walk up to the gate, and tug on one of the knotted loops.

"Hold your horses," says a metallic-sounding voice, as a zany-looking droid pops into the ticket window. "Your mind is your ticket to the MathZone," it says. "To open the naughty knotty gate, just find the knot that is not a knot. When you untangle it, the gate will unlock."

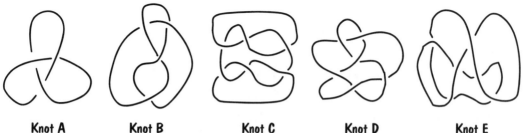

Knot A   Knot B   Knot C   Knot D   Knot E

Which one of these tangles is not a true knot?

You study the five knotted loops, wondering which one you ought to try to untangle. Can you figure out which loop is not a knot?

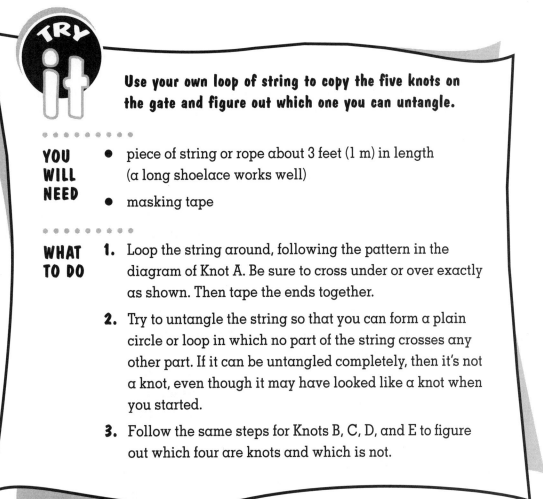

Use your own loop of string to copy the five knots on the gate and figure out which one you can untangle.

YOU WILL NEED

- piece of string or rope about 3 feet (1 m) in length (a long shoelace works well)
- masking tape

WHAT TO DO

1. Loop the string around, following the pattern in the diagram of Knot A. Be sure to cross under or over exactly as shown. Then tape the ends together.

2. Try to untangle the string so that you can form a plain circle or loop in which no part of the string crosses any other part. If it can be untangled completely, then it's not a knot, even though it may have looked like a knot when you started.

3. Follow the same steps for Knots B, C, D, and E to figure out which four are knots and which is not.

[Answer on p. 99.]

Knots and Unknots

Have you ever watched a magician tie a gigantic knot then magically make it fall apart? Sometimes what looks like a very impressive knot isn't a knot at all. Magicians and escape artists are experts at tying phony knots.

Mathematicians are especially interested in knots that can never be undone. Mathematically, a **knot** is a one-dimensional curve that winds through itself in three-dimensional space and catches its own tail to form a loop. You can untie a shoelace and untangle a fishing line, but you can't untie or get rid of the knot in a mathematician's knotted loop. To turn a tangled shoelace into a mathematical knot, you would have to tape the shoelace's ends together. Then you wouldn't be able to untie the knot.

If a loop has no knot in it and can be made tangle free to look like a circle, mathematicians call it an **unknot.** Only one of the tangled loops on the MathZone gate is an unknot.

To Be or Knot to Be

Knot theorists are mathematicians who look for patterns that distinguish true knots from messy tangles called unknots, which can come apart when shaken. Knot theorists also look for ways to classify different types of knots.

How many different knots can you make? To tell one from another, you can start putting them into groups by counting how many times the rope or cord crosses itself. To make it easier to count, lay each knotted loop down on a table.

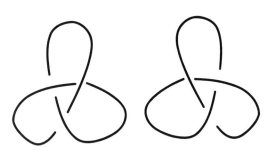

A trefoil knot has three crossings. The trefoil knot on the right is the mirror image of the trefoil knot on the left.

Knot A on the MathZone gate is called a **trefoil knot.** With only three crossings, it's the simplest type of knot there is. In the top left diagram, the trefoil knot on the right is a mirror image of the trefoil knot on the left. Are they both the same knot? No. There's nothing you can do to make one knot exactly like the other without cutting the loop, rearranging the strand, and joining the ends again (unless you look at it in a mirror).

Knot B on the MathZone gate is the only type of knot that crosses itself four times. Mathematicians call it the "figure-8" knot. Knot C has six crossings. Most people know it as the familiar "granny knot." A square knot also has six crossings. Are a square knot and a granny knot the same knot? Look at the crossing pattern for each knot to the left. Do you see the two places where the knots differ?

Both the granny knot (left) and the square knot (right) have six crossings. The two knots are not the same, however, because their crossing patterns differ.

Mathematicians have identified 1,701,936 different knots with 16 or fewer crossings. It was very tricky for them to come up with the list because sometimes two knots can look different but really be the same. At other times, a tangle that looks like a knot is really an unknot.

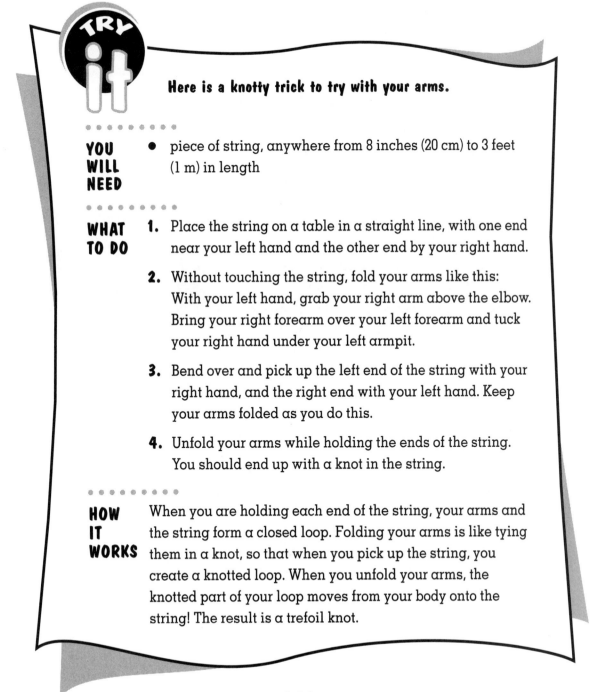

TRY it

Here is a knotty trick to try with your arms.

YOU WILL NEED

- piece of string, anywhere from 8 inches (20 cm) to 3 feet (1 m) in length

WHAT TO DO

1. Place the string on a table in a straight line, with one end near your left hand and the other end by your right hand.

2. Without touching the string, fold your arms like this: With your left hand, grab your right arm above the elbow. Bring your right forearm over your left forearm and tuck your right hand under your left armpit.

3. Bend over and pick up the left end of the string with your right hand, and the right end with your left hand. Keep your arms folded as you do this.

4. Unfold your arms while holding the ends of the string. You should end up with a knot in the string.

HOW IT WORKS

When you are holding each end of the string, your arms and the string form a closed loop. Folding your arms is like tying them in a knot, so that when you pick up the string, you create a knotted loop. When you unfold your arms, the knotted part of your loop moves from your body onto the string! The result is a trefoil knot.

Here's an example of a loop that looks knotted but really isn't. Magicians sometimes use loops like this one in their tricks.

To keep from getting fooled, mathematicians have worked out some formulas that can serve as shortcuts for telling a knot from an unknot and one knot from another. They're still searching for a single formula that identifies all possible knots.

KNOTS IN YOUR BODY

Would you believe that when you catch a cold or the flu, your body could be getting tied up in knots?

Scientists are using the mathematical study of knots to help understand the long, skinny, twisted loops and links of DNA, or deoxyribonucleic acid—the molecules that determine the genetic code for every living thing. If a single DNA strand were magnified to become as wide as a telephone wire, it would be more than a mile (more than a kilometer) long. Heaps of DNA strands sit like microscopic spaghetti inside plant and animal cells. Those strands may be twisted around one another, joined together to form loops, or tied in knots.

Molecular biologists have discovered that when a virus attacks living cells, it can break up unknotted loops of DNA, then rejoin the strands to form knots. Biologists and mathematicians are now working together to use knot theory as a way to figure out how viruses work. That could lead to a cure for certain diseases—maybe even a cure for the common cold!

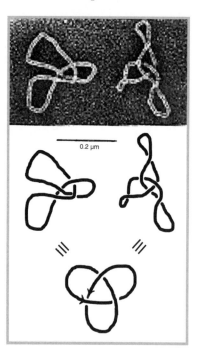

The two tangled loops of DNA, as seen under an electron microscope (top), both turn out to be trefoil knots (bottom).

Cat's Cradle

Have you ever played cat's cradle? You can use a loop made from about 6 feet (2 m) of nylon cord or other smooth string. Hang the loop on your thumbs, and pick up the loop with your little fingers, so that the string goes across the palms of your hands, like this:

Cat's cradle starts with a loop of string
held as shown between your hands.

Then slip each index finger under the string on the opposite palm and pull your hands apart. You can loop your fingers in and out of the string in different ways to form various knotlike designs. No

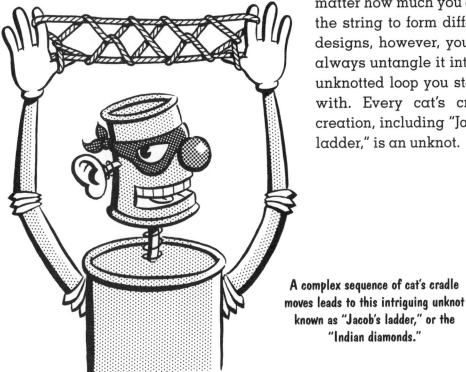

matter how much you cross the string to form different designs, however, you can always untangle it into the unknotted loop you started with. Every cat's cradle creation, including "Jacob's ladder," is an unknot.

A complex sequence of cat's cradle moves leads to this intriguing unknot known as "Jacob's ladder," or the "Indian diamonds."

Lord Kelvin's Knots

Mathematicians originally got the idea of studying knots from William Thomson, known as Lord Kelvin. Lord Kelvin was a famous physicist who lived more than 100 years ago in England. At that time, scientists didn't know that atoms consisted of particles called electrons, protons, and neutrons. They did, however, suspect that atoms of oxygen, hydrogen, iron, sulfur, and other elements were not exactly alike because of their different chemical behavior.

Lord Kelvin suggested that atoms might be like little whirlpools in an invisible fluid that fills all space. He proposed that different elements would correspond to different knotted tubes of fluid whirling in closed loops. For example, atoms of the simplest element, hydrogen, might look like a trefoil knot, and those of other elements might look like other knots. Inspired by that theory, mathematicians started to make tables of all possible types of knots.

Mathematicians continue to study knots, although Lord Kelvin's theory turned out to be wrong. We now know that there is no invisible fluid filling all space and that the number of protons in the nucleus of an atom is what decides which element it is. Lord Kelvin still made a name for himself in science for several discoveries and inventions, including the Kelvin temperature scale, which was later named for him.

The MapZone

Taking hold of the unknot that you untangled on the MathZone gate, you tug on the loop of rope. The gate slowly swings open.

You find yourself in a mad swirl of activity: clamoring crowds, dinging bells, and roaring machines. You step up to a nearby booth decorated with brightly colored maps and labeled with a bold sign.

"Come and get your MathZone map," calls a woman wearing star-studded sunglasses and a colorful vest that looks like a map of the world. She unfolds a big sheet, revealing a map outlined in black ink on white paper. The woman hands it to you. "This is your guide to all the MathZone activities," she says. "Before you venture on, try solving the Map-ematical challenge."

She hands you six colored pencils. "Try to figure out the smallest number of colors you need to fill in the MathZone map so that you can easily see a distinctive color for each activity area," she says. "Use the fewest possible colors, and you will win a can of Fractal Soda! One rule: No two sections that share a border may be the same color."

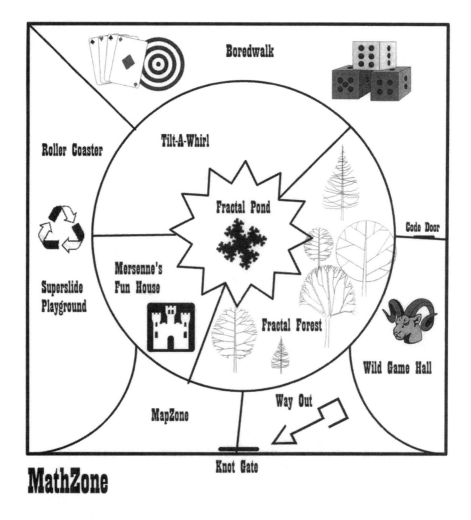

Can you complete the map using six colors? Five? Four? Three?

Make copies of black-and-white maps, then see how many colors you need to fill them in.

YOU WILL NEED

- set of six colored pencils, crayons, or felt-tip markers
- three copies of the MathZone map, page 10
- three copies of United States map, page 12

WHAT TO DO

1. Color one of your copies of the MathZone map so that no two activity zones sharing a border have the same color. Do you need all six colors?

2. Try coloring a second MathZone map using fewer colors than you used the first time. For example, if you used all six colors to complete the first map, use five this time.

3. Can you color the third MathZone map with even fewer colors? What seems to be the smallest number of colors you need to complete the map?

4. Now try it with a more complex map. In a map of the United States, how many colors do you need if you want to avoid using the same color for any states that share a border? (A point is not a border, so you may use the same color for states such as Utah and New Mexico.)

Guess how many colors you would need to complete any possible map! Many mathematicians spent decades trying to answer that very question.

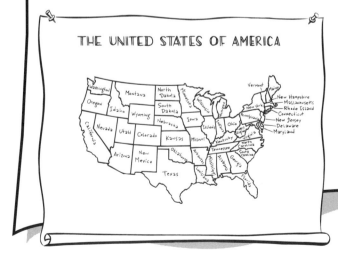

THE UNITED STATES OF AMERICA

[Answer follows.]

THE UNITED STATES OF AMERICA

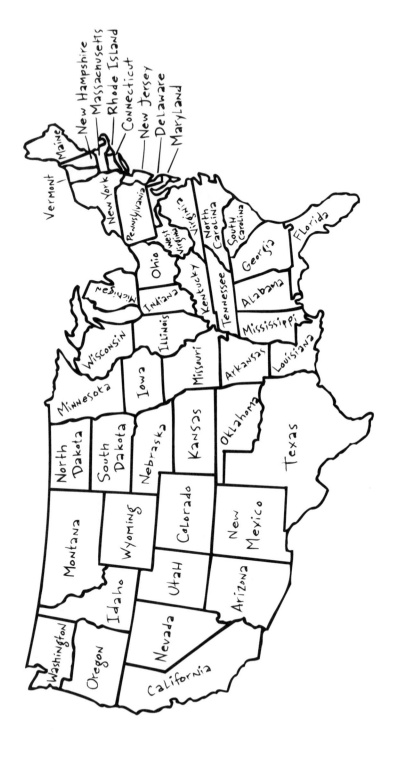

Map-ematical Solutions

You may have figured out that you need at least four colors to complete the MathZone map. You could almost do it with three colors. In the area around Fractal Pond, however, the central region shares a border with three other zones.

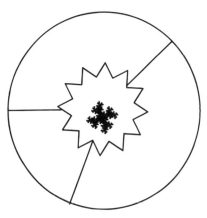

In the middle of the MathZone map, the area around Fractal Pond (shown in black) shares a border with three other zones.

Here is one way to complete the MathZone map using four colors.

You also need four colors to complete the U.S. map. It is almost possible to color all the states with just three colors. Can you figure out which two states make a fourth color necessary? Hint: Look for states surrounded by an odd number of neighboring states.

[Answer on p. 99.]

• • •

A map of South America has the same problem. Look how Peru, Brazil, Paraguay, Argentina, and Chile completely surround Bolivia on a map of South America. Three countries surround Paraguay.

Because Bolivia and Paraguay are surrounded by an odd number of countries, it takes four colors to complete a map of South America.

Challenge: Suppose you are using the colors red, blue, green, and yellow. Try to color the U.S. map so that it has as few yellows as possible. Can you get it down to just two states colored yellow?

[Answer on p. 99.]

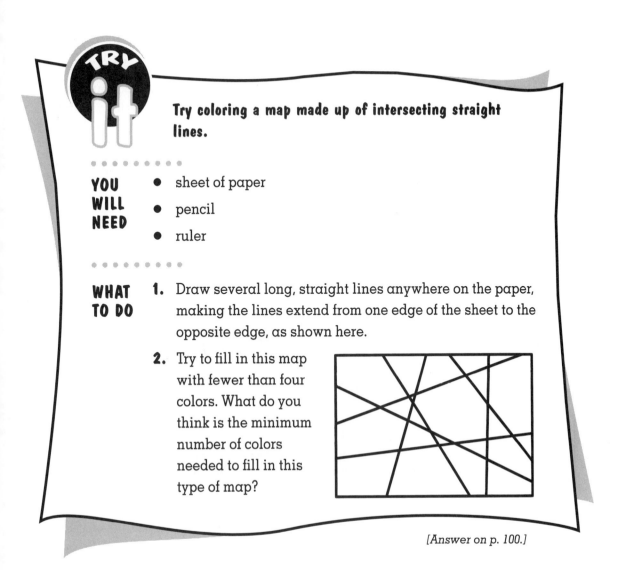

[Answer on p. 100.]

Simple Maps, Complex Math

It has taken more than a hundred years for mathematicians to prove that four colors are always enough to complete every conceivable map that can be drawn on a flat piece of paper, with no neighboring territories sharing the same color.

The problem was first posed in a letter that Francis Guthrie, a student in England, wrote to his younger brother, Frederick, in 1852. Frederick, in turn, described the problem to his college math instructor, the prominent British mathematician Augustus De Morgan. The problem intrigued De Morgan, and he quickly realized that it wasn't as simple to solve as it sounded. Word of the four-color-map problem spread quickly.

Another English mathematician, Charles Lutwidge Dodgson, worked on the four-color-map problem. Dodgson figured out that four colors would be needed for the type of map shown below, which resembles the area around Fractal Pond on the MathZone map and the area around Luxembourg on a map of western Europe. (Later in this chapter, you'll find out how the map-loving Dodgson delighted countless children around the world.)

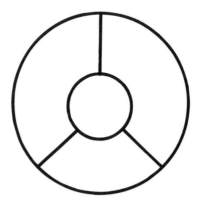

Four colors are always needed for a map in
which three regions surround a fourth area.

In 1879, Alfred Bray Kempe, a British lawyer and amateur mathematician, announced that he had found a step-by-step map-coloring procedure guaranteeing that no more than four colors would be needed for any map. His argument was convincing, but 11 years later, someone found a loophole. There were a few, special, complicated cases that Kempe's method did not cover.

Finally, in 1976, two math professors at the University of Illinois, Kenneth Appel and Wolfgang Haken, came up with a proof of the four-color-map theorem. One of the biggest problems in mathematics had finally been solved! Mathematicians around the world cheered and celebrated.

Anyone who tried to study the proof was in for a shock, however. It was one of the longest mathematical proofs that anyone had ever come up with. The writing and diagrams filled hundreds of pages. It was the first time mathematicians had ever relied on a computer to calculate and verify certain facts needed for their proof.

The computer allowed Appel and Haken to analyze a huge number of possible types of maps. If anyone had tried to do the job by hand, it would have taken almost forever.

Even now, some mathematicians still wonder whether there might be a tiny error in the proof. The complex computer software could have been faulty, or the method of mathematical reasoning could have been flawed. The general consensus, however, is that the proof is probably correct.

Some day, someone may find a shorter proof, but it's possible that there really is no easier way to prove the four-color-map theorem. Sometimes a short, simple mathematical idea calls for an incredibly complicated proof.

· ·

LEWIS CARROLL: AUTHOR, MATHEMATICIAN

'Contrariwise,' continued Tweedledee, 'if it was so,
it might be; and if it were so, it would be:
but as it isn't, it ain't. That's logic.'

Through the Looking-Glass

'Let me see: four times five is twelve, and four times
six is thirteen, and four times seven is—oh dear!
I shall never get to twenty at that rate!'

Alice's Adventures in Wonderland

Why would the author of a fantasy about falling down a rabbit hole spend time tackling the four-color-map problem?

The person who wrote under the pen name of Lewis Carroll was actually Charles Lutwidge Dodgson, the map-ematical mathematician mentioned earlier. Dodgson, who taught at Christ Church College in Oxford, England, especially enjoyed mathematical puzzles, games, and magic tricks. He would often perform magic tricks for children and carry around mechanical puzzles for them to solve. Dodgson's interest in card games and chess provided the background for the Lewis Carroll books *Alice's Adventures in Wonderland* and *Through the Looking-Glass*.

Another of Dodgson's books, *Pillow Problems,* is a collection of math problems that Dodgson solved in his head while lying awake at night. He found that thinking about math problems in bed was a great way to get the day's worries off his mind before falling asleep.

The Crazy Roller Coaster

Y ou show the map woman your four-color MathZone map. She hands you a coupon for a free can of Fractal Soda. With a cryptic smile, she says, "See you at the races."

Time to explore! Gaping at the crowds and the popcorn stands, listening to the rumble of the nearby Tilt-A-Whirl and the

JESSICA WOLK-STANLEY '99

screams of riders spinning wildly, you again wonder why this, of all places, is called the MathZone. Mathematics is quiet and orderly, but this place is as noisy and chaotic as any amusement park.

"Sodas, popcorn, right this way," shouts a vendor wearing a black top hat decorated with lavender snowflakes. You give him your coupon. He hands you a can painted with a cool blue-and-white snowflake pattern. You sit down, sip the refreshing ice-cold soda, and study your MathZone map.

Near the section labeled "Roller Coaster," you spot a recycling symbol on the map. It looks like three bent arrows chasing one another around a trian-gular loop. You notice the same symbol printed on your soda can. Savoring the last sip, you decide to head toward the roller coaster to look for a place to recycle the empty can.

Soon you come to a row of bins marked with recycling sym-bols. You drop your soda can into the bin labeled "aluminum only."

"Race you to the Superslide," someone shouts, as a group of kids runs past you over to a nearby play-ground. The boys and girls begin sliding around on a weird sculpture of twisted metal. Everyone is having such a blast that you decide to head over.

You climb onto the Superslide and slip down its inside surface, speeding along the bottom, then slowing to a halt across from your starting point. You pull yourself up to the top and climb onto the out-side surface. You whip down a twisty curve, sailing onto a big pile of wood chips.

The Superslide has a strange, twisted surface.

You find that you can slide on both the outside and the inside of the Superslide. You run your hand all the way along the smooth metal surface. As it travels along the surface, your hand mysteriously passes from the inside to the outside of the looping slide, then back to the inside.

You hear the rumble of the roller coaster and a sudden burst of shrieks. You look up and see a speeding train full of riders turn upside down as the track loops upward. Continuing along the curved track, the riders find themselves right-side up again.

This roller coaster is a little different, though. Instead of the steep hills and valleys found on most roller coasters, the track loops around like a twisted circle. In fact, it looks curiously similar to the twisty Superslide. It also looks like a huge recycling symbol!

This unusual roller coaster has a twist, making it a Möbius band.

As you head over for a closer look, the train of riders rumbles toward the finish line at the bottom of the loop. But when the train slows to a stop at the bottom, everyone is upside down again!

"This roller coaster is on a math track, designed by the MathZone topologist," announces a woman in a green T-shirt with a big white recycling symbol on the front. She pulls a lever and the train starts moving again. "Don't worry folks," she says. "You're all going to end up right-side up!"

How do the riders manage to reach the finish line right-side up?

[Answer follows.]

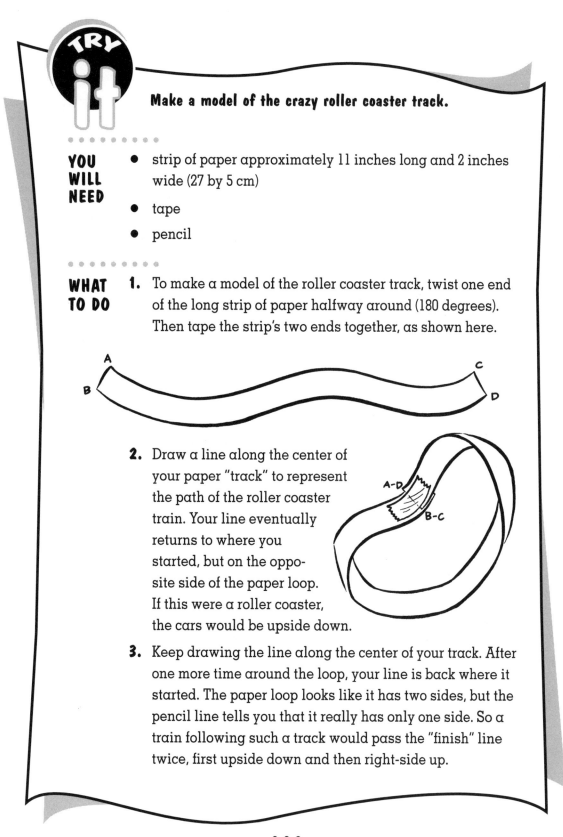

Make a model of the crazy roller coaster track.

YOU WILL NEED

- strip of paper approximately 11 inches long and 2 inches wide (27 by 5 cm)
- tape
- pencil

WHAT TO DO

1. To make a model of the roller coaster track, twist one end of the long strip of paper halfway around (180 degrees). Then tape the strip's two ends together, as shown here.

2. Draw a line along the center of your paper "track" to represent the path of the roller coaster train. Your line eventually returns to where you started, but on the opposite side of the paper loop. If this were a roller coaster, the cars would be upside down.

3. Keep drawing the line along the center of your track. After one more time around the loop, your line is back where it started. The paper loop looks like it has two sides, but the pencil line tells you that it really has only one side. So a train following such a track would pass the "finish" line twice, first upside down and then right-side up.

Möbius Madness

The roller coaster track, the playground Superslide, and the recycling symbol are all in the form of a **Möbius strip,** or band. This curious shape was discovered by German mathematician and astronomer August Möbius in 1858.

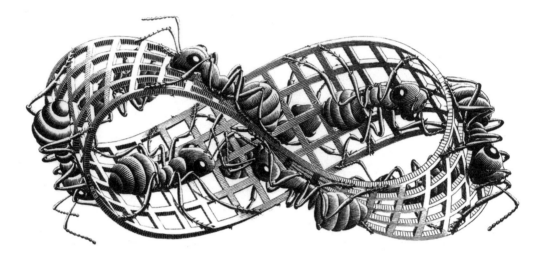

This drawing by the artist M. C. Escher shows ants crawling endlessly along a Möbius strip.

An important branch of twentieth-century mathematics, known as **topology,** grew from Möbius's description of how a shape that appears two-sided can really be one-sided. Sometimes described as rubber-sheet geometry, topology is the study of the features that various shapes have in common, even when those shapes are twisted or stretched in different ways.

To a topologist, for example, a coffee mug and a doughnut are really the same thing (though one is certainly tastier than the other). It's possible to imagine expanding a coffee cup's handle while shrinking its bowl until all that's left is a fat ring.

Here's how a topologist might turn a coffee cup into a doughnut.

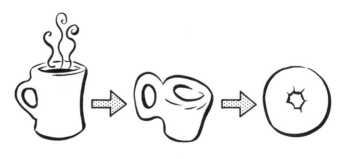

So topologists focus on features (such as the number of holes, sides, or edges) that survive after shapes are bent, stretched, and twisted, but not torn. Ideas from topology, from classifying shapes to detecting geometric similarities, have turned out to be useful in designing roads and buildings, untangling how the human body works, and determining the shape of the universe.

The Möbius band is one of the simplest of the many surfaces and shapes that topologists study. Here's a more complex (and weird) surface, called a **Klein bottle:**

A Klein bottle has only one side and one surface.

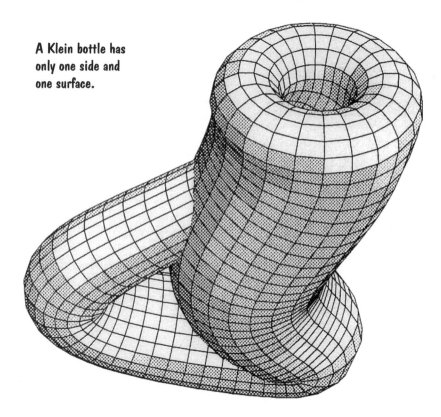

The Möbius band is a shape that has just one surface and one edge. A sphere has no edge, but two surfaces (an inside and an outside surface). A Klein bottle has no edges and only one surface (the inside and the outside are both part of the same surface!).

Turn yourself into a Möbius band.

1. Stick your arms out in front of you and touch the tips of your two thumbs together, the tips of each index finger, each middle finger, and so on.

2. Now turn one hand halfway around, keeping only your two middle fingers together. Touch each thumb to your little finger on the opposite hand, and each index finger to the ring finger on the opposite hand.

3. Study the loop you've made, and you will realize it's a Möbius band!

Here is a magic trick you can perform with a Möbius band.

- Möbius band from the activity on page 23.
- pair of scissors

1. Divide the Möbius band into two tracks by cutting along the line you drew down its center. You should end up with a band that's longer, thinner, and more twisted than your original Möbius band.

2. Cut along the center of this new band. It will turn into two twisted bands that are intertwined.

HELAMAN FERGUSON: SCULPTOR, MATHEMATICIAN

Most mathematicians do their work on paper or on a computer, but Helaman Ferguson uses bronze and stone. Ferguson works as a mathematician for a computer software company. Most of the time, however, he's a sculptor who uses mathematical equations to help carve mind-boggling topological shapes into works of art you can touch. He even makes out-of-this-world play equipment for children to climb on and explore.

Using special equipment, Ferguson translates geometric forms drawn on a computer screen into instructions for carving stone and other materials in just the right spots to create his mathematical sculptures.

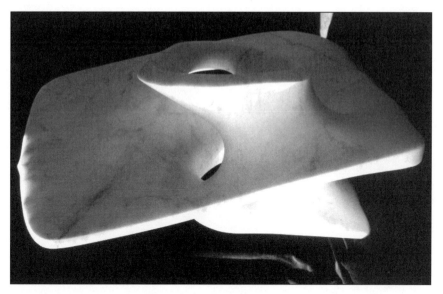

Using formulas for a new shape discovered by Brazilian mathematician Celso Costa, Ferguson has created this graceful sculpture in marble. He hopes to make a 10-foot-wide fiberglass version for kids to touch and explore at a science museum.

Mersenne's Fun House

Puzzler:	Why is Trek 4 missing?
Hint:	Why are Treks 6, 8, 9, and 10 also missing? Read on for more clues. *[Answer on p. 100.]*

"**O**uch!" screams the first stair, as you start to climb a rickety set of steps, heading toward a stone structure that looks like a medieval castle.

"Crruuuunch," goes the second stair. When you set foot on the third stair, a loud buzzer goes off. The fourth stair is perfectly quiet. As you step on stair five, an evil laugh sends shivers down your spine.

Quickly, you step to the sixth stair: Silence again. Seventh stair: A weird weeping sound. Eighth stair: Silence. Ninth: Silence again. Tenth: More silence. Eleventh: Crash!!!!

In a panic, you jump to the stair labeled 12: Silence. Then up to 13: Booming thunder!!! Steps 14, 15, and 16 are silent. Dare you try step 17? Slowly, slowly . . .

BOOM! A cannon goes off, and you leap to 18 (silence), then to 19 (a drum roll), and finally you reach the top. You see a hefty wooden door with the number 93 painted on it. Above the door is a sign.

You knock, but there is no answer. You try turning the knob, but the door is locked. To your right is another door, labeled 95. You try the knob, but this door is locked, too. You step to the left and try door number 91. Locked.

"Very odd," you think, gazing up and down a row of 17 doors, each labeled with an odd number. You walk back over to the right and try door 97. Voilà! It opens.

Wwwooooooooo! A ghostlike howl greets you. Hesitant but curious, you step into a hallway and find 13 black curtains hanging from one of the walls. You peek behind a curtain labeled 117 and find only a blank wall. You try curtain 119. Another blank wall.

Feeling baffled, you glance around the hallway and happen to notice a U.S. map hanging on the wall behind you—in four colors, of course. Below it is the familiar quote: "One nation under God, _____, with liberty and justice for all."

While trying to think of the missing word, you stare back at the row of curtains. You wonder if curtain 123, 125, 127, or 129 has anything other than a blank wall behind it.

Which curtain is your best bet?

[Answer on p. 100.]

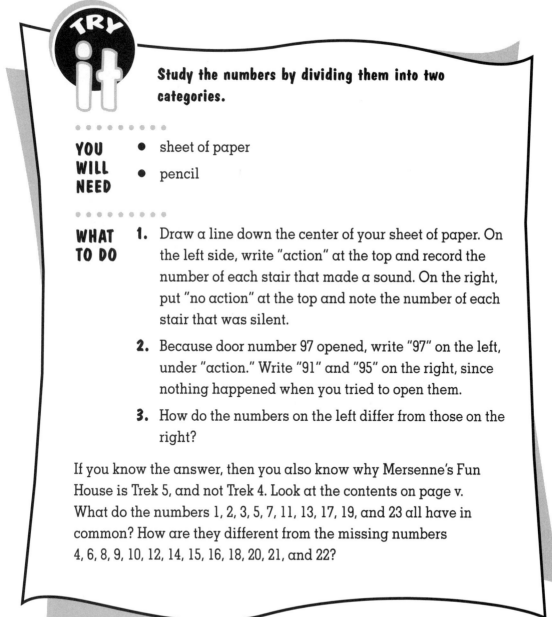

Study the numbers by dividing them into two categories.

YOU WILL NEED

- sheet of paper
- pencil

WHAT TO DO

1. Draw a line down the center of your sheet of paper. On the left side, write "action" at the top and record the number of each stair that made a sound. On the right, put "no action" at the top and note the number of each stair that was silent.

2. Because door number 97 opened, write "97" on the left, under "action." Write "91" and "95" on the right, since nothing happened when you tried to open them.

3. How do the numbers on the left differ from those on the right?

If you know the answer, then you also know why Mersenne's Fun House is Trek 5, and not Trek 4. Look at the contents on page v. What do the numbers 1, 2, 3, 5, 7, 11, 13, 17, 19, and 23 all have in common? How are they different from the missing numbers 4, 6, 8, 9, 10, 12, 14, 15, 16, 18, 20, 21, and 22?

[Answer on p. 100.]

Sieve of Eratosthenes

By now, you may have figured out that the key to making your way around the Fun House is to find the prime numbers.

Prime numbers are *indivisible* (like the United States). If a number can't be evenly divided by any number except 1 and the number itself, then it is a prime. If a number is divisible, the numbers it can be divided by are called *factors*. Numbers that are not primes are called **composite numbers.**

Around 300 B.C., the Greek mathematician Euclid proved that there is an infinite number of primes. There are four primes—2, 3, 5, and 7—among the first ten integers (1, 2, 3, 4, 5, 6, 7, 8, 9, 10). The number 1 is defined as being neither prime nor composite. As the numbers get larger, the primes are fewer and farther apart.

There are 25 primes among the first 100 integers, 21 primes among the next 100 integers (101 to 200), and 16 among the next 100 integers (201 to 300). Even though the primes look like they would eventually peter out, any long enough sequence of integers will have prime numbers lurking among the composite numbers.

Finding prime numbers has long been a favorite pastime of mathematicians. Because primes are scattered among whole numbers in seemingly unpredictable ways, they can be hard to catch. The sieve of Eratosthenes (pronounced "air-uh-TOSS-thin-neez"), discovered in the third century B.C. by the Greek mathematician Eratosthenes of Cyrene, generates a list of primes by eliminating the composite numbers.

For example, to find all the primes between 1 and 100, you write down all the whole numbers up to 100. Following a special procedure, you then cross out the numbers that are not prime, so that only the primes are left.

Use the sieve of Eratosthenes to find the primes.

YOU WILL NEED

- pencil
- grid shown below

1	2	3	4	5	6	7	8	9	10
11	12	13	14	15	16	17	18	19	20
21	22	23	24	25	26	27	28	29	30
31	32	33	34	35	36	37	38	39	40
41	42	43	44	45	46	47	48	49	50
51	52	53	54	55	56	57	58	59	60
61	62	63	64	65	66	67	68	69	70
71	72	73	74	75	76	77	78	79	80
81	82	83	84	85	86	87	88	89	90
91	92	93	94	95	96	97	98	99	100

WHAT TO DO

1. Circle the first prime, which is 2. Now cross out all multiples of two (4, 6, 8, and so on).

2. Circle the next prime, which is 3. Cross out all multiples of three (6, 9, 12, 15, 18, . . .).

3. Circle the next unmarked prime, which is 5. Cross out all multiples of 5.

4. The next unmarked prime is 7. Circle it and cross out the multiples of 7.

That finishes the job because the next prime is 11. The multiples of 11 appearing on the chart are 22, 33, 44, 55, 66, 77, 88, and 99. All of those have already been crossed out, however. Multiples of 13, 17, and so on, have also been crossed out.

Circle the remaining prime numbers. The sieve ends up trapping 25 numbers—the 25 primes among the integers from 1 to 100.

[Answer on p. 100.]

PRIME PATTERNS

Mathematicians have found many interesting patterns involving primes, but no foolproof way of predicting their locations. Here is an intriguing list of primes:

31

331

3,331

33,331

333,331

3,333,331

33,333,331

Does the pattern keep on going? Alas, no. The number 333,333,331 is not prime because $333,333,331 = 17 \times 19,607,843$.

Back to the Fun House

Among the four curtains you are contemplating in Mersenne's Fun House, two curtains—numbers 123 and 129—are both divisible by 3. The third number, 125, is divisible by 5. When you cast your sieve of Eratosthenes over the numbers between 101 and 200, however, you soon discover that the number 127 is a prime.

You draw aside curtain 127. Instead of encountering a blank wall, you find yourself standing at the top of 11 long, hilly wooden slides. The slides are numbered 201, 203, 205, 207, 211, 213, 215, 217, 219, 221, and 223. By now, you know to look for a prime number. Which one will you choose? (There are two primes in this sequence. Choose either.)

[Answer on p. 101.]

You whiz down the long, hilly slide and land in a hall with seven mirrors. When you gaze into mirror number 295, it makes you look very short. Mirror 297 makes you look tall. In mirror 299, you look fat; in 301, you look skinny; in 303, you are upside down; and in 305, your body is turned sideways. Finally, you find yourself looking perfectly normal in mirror 307.

You stand staring into mirror 307, making sure you still have two eyes, two ears, and ten fingers. Suddenly, a trap door falls open beneath your feet. Slowly, you sink down and land in a stone room with five candles and three stained-glass windows. Two computers are on a table. A bearded man in a long, brown robe sits studying one of the computer screens.

"Voilà! Fantastique!" he exclaims, still staring at the screen. Then he turns to you and explains in a French accent, "I have found a 19-digit prime!" He stands up and offers his hand.

"Bonjour. Mersenne is my name. Welcome to my Fun House."

As you shake hands with him, you notice little black numbers printed up and down his robe.

"Since you found your way to my cell, you must know about primes," Mersenne continues. "You have been finding small primes all around the Fun House. To hunt for very large primes, you need a computer.

"Have a seat," he offers, pointing to the chair in front of his second computer. "I will show you a fascinating new computer game: The Great Internet Mersenne Prime Search."

Are you game?

Mersenne Primes

The largest known prime numbers are found among *Mersenne numbers*, named for Marin Mersenne (pronounced "mare-SEN"), a French priest who taught mathematics, theology, philosophy, and music during the early 1600s. Mersenne was especially interested in prime numbers. He tried to find a mathematical formula that would represent all primes.

Marin Mersenne was a seventeenth-century priest who studied prime numbers.

Although he failed to find such a formula (and, of course, didn't have a computer), Mersenne became well known for his work on a certain type of prime. What we now call a **Mersenne number** is two multiplied by itself a certain number of times, minus one. In other words, a Mersenne number is two to any power, minus one. For example:

$$2 \times 2 - 1 = 2^2 - 1 = 3$$

$$2^3 - 1 = 7$$

$$2^4 - 1 = 15$$

$$2^5 - 1 = 31$$

$$2^6 - 1 = 63$$

$$2^7 - 1 = 127$$

The numbers 3, 7, 15, 31, 63, and 127 are all Mersenne numbers. Four of those (3, 7, 31, and 127) also happen to be prime, so they are called **Mersenne primes.** When you opened curtain 127, you didn't just find a prime. You found a Mersenne prime.

Mersenne himself was aware of those four Mersenne primes and three others:

$$2^{13} - 1 = 8,191$$

$$2^{17} - 1 = 131,071$$

$$2^{19} - 1 = 524,287$$

He claimed that $2^{31} - 1$ is prime, but no one was able to prove it —until 1772. Mersenne also claimed that $2^{67} - 1$ and $2^{257} - 1$ are prime, but he was later proved wrong.

By 1914, mathematicians had discovered four more Mersenne primes, the longest of which is 39 digits long!

Computers have taken over the search for Mersenne primes since 1952, when mathematicians used an early type of computer to find five more Mersenne primes. Each of those five primes is hundreds of digits long.

In 1978, two high school students in California—Laura Nickel and Curt Landon Noll—used a large computer to set the record for the highest known prime of that time. Their number, $2^{21,701} - 1$, was the twenty-fifth Mersenne prime discovered. It has 6,533 digits.

After that, the pursuit of primes quickly became a private game for the largest and fastest supercomputers. That changed in 1996, however, when a remarkable new project allowed home computer users to join the search for primes.

The Great Internet Mersenne Prime Search (GIMPS) is a project started by George Woltman, a computer programmer in Florida. It has brought together more than 4,000 volunteers in a systematic effort to check Mersenne numbers to see which are primes. Participants range from school kids to computer professionals.

In January 1998, Roland Clarkson, a college student in California, set a new record for finding the largest known Mersenne prime. Working with the GIMPS project, Clarkson got his personal computer to prove that $2^{3,021,377} - 1$ is prime. The newfound prime, which has 909,526 digits, is the thirty-seventh known Mersenne prime.

GOLDBACH'S CONJECTURES

In 1742, Christian Goldbach, a Prussian mathematician, sent a letter to Swiss mathematician Leonhard Euler suggesting that any even number greater than 2 can be written as the sum of two primes. The number 32, for example, is the sum of 13 and 19. No one has yet proved that this is true for all even numbers.

Goldbach also suggested that any odd number greater than 5 can be expressed as the sum of three primes. For example, the number 33 is the sum of 23, 7, and 3. Mathematicians have come close to proving this.

In both of the preceding conjectures, the same prime may be used more than once in a sum. For example, 6 = 3 + 3 and 17 = 5 + 5 + 7.

The Fractal Pond Race

Exiting the mind-bending Fun House through door number 331, you find yourself at the edge of a thick forest. Trees with bare, knobby branches straggle among tall, cone-shaped evergreens. Jagged rocks, rotting logs, and fallen pinecones lie scattered about the hilly terrain. Luscious green ferns dot the

Jessica Wolk-Stanley '99

forest floor. A winding path leads into the forest. A sign with an arrow points the way.

You study your MathZone map and realize that you are walking through the Fractal Forest toward Fractal Pond.

As you set out on the path, the billowing white clouds above start to turn thick and gray. Large, soft snowflakes begin to fall. Brushing the snow off your jacket sleeves, you notice how each tiny snowflake appears to have its own intricate shape.

As the snowfall tapers off, you come to a sunny clearing with a small pond bordered by a sandy beach. Surrounding the beach is a two-lane oval racetrack. On the inside lane, you spot a gray tortoise poised behind a line marked "start." The outside lane looks empty, except for a small black speck at the starting line. Off to the side sits a crowd of spectators.

"Come see the race," beckons a woman with star-shaped sunglasses. You recognize her from the MapZone booth, but she is wearing a jacket over her colorful map vest. The jacket has the same snowflake design that was on your can of Fractal Soda.

You sit down and study the race course, which circles the pond and ends just behind the starting line. At the line marked "finish" sit a head of lettuce and a sugar cube. A glass wall between the start and the finish lines prevents racers from going backward directly to the finish line.

"The first race will now begin," roars a rotund official. Dressed in white and black, he looks like a squat snowman with warts all over his body. "On your marks. . . . Get set. . . . Go!"

The tortoise slowly crosses the starting line and begins creeping along its lane. Instantly, the tiny black speck zips past the tortoise, racing in the outside lane. You recognize the spindly shape of an ant! While the tortoise lumbers along, the little ant zooms around the pond and climbs onto the sugar cube.

"And the ant wins, hands down!" yells the awesome snowman, as the crowd cheers. Tediously, the tortoise inches its way around to the lettuce.

"Now for the fractal race!" the snowman announces. He coaxes the ant and the tortoise across the sandy beach, over to the water's edge. Then he places the tortoise behind a new starting line, with its left legs in the water and its right legs on the dry, sandy shore. He puts the ant just in front of its reptilian rival, also at the water's edge.

"In this race there is a special rule," the snowman explains. "The racers must keep their left legs wet and their right legs dry as they circle the pond."

Who do you bet will win?

[Answer follows.]

Deceiving Distances

Like the edges of many lakes and the seacoasts of many countries, the shoreline of Fractal Pond is not a simple, smooth curve. It weaves in and out in accordance with the contours of the sandy shore.

Examine any natural shore closely enough, and you will find that each individual ridge and inlet is also composed of smaller ridges and inlets. Each of those ridges and inlets is in turn composed of even tinier ridges and inlets, and so on.

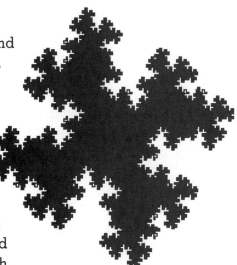

Fractal Pond has large bays, and those bays have inlets, and the inlets in turn have even smaller inlets, creating a highly indented shoreline.

When the race at Fractal Pond begins, the ant hurries along in front. As the tortoise sets off leisurely, however, it steps right over the ant and soon takes the lead. Because of its relatively large size, the tortoise can circle the pond following a fairly simple path while keeping its left legs in the water.

The speedy ant, however, has to race back and forth along tiny meanderings of the shoreline in order to keep its left legs wet. The ant ends up having to travel a far greater distance, so the slow and steady tortoise wins the race around Fractal Pond!

COASTING ALONG

Maps of a rugged coastline illustrate a curious property of features that repeat themselves on smaller and smaller scales. The curves can wiggle so much that it's hard to come up with a measurement of a coastline's length! Finer and finer scales reveal more and more detail and lead to longer and longer coastline lengths.

Here is an example.

- On a world globe, the eastern coast of the United States looks like a fairly smooth line that stretches somewhere between 2,000 and 3,000 miles (3,200 to 4,800 kilometers) from the northern coast of Maine to the southern tip of Florida.

- The same coast on an atlas page showing only the United States looks much more ragged. Adding in the lengths of capes and bays, the length of the coast measures 4,000 to 5,000 miles (6,400 to 8,000 kilometers).

- Piecing together detailed regional charts to create a giant coastal map would reveal an incredibly complex curve from Maine to Florida that may be 10,000 to 12,000 miles (16,000 to 19,000 kilometers) long.

- A person walking along the shoreline, staying within a step of the water's edge, would have to scramble more than 15,000 miles (24,000 kilometers) to get from Maine to the bottom of Florida.

- A determined ant taking the same coastline expedition but staying only an ant step away from the water might have to travel about 30,000 miles (48,000 kilometers)!

As your steps get shorter, the total distance traveled along a ragged coastline grows longer.

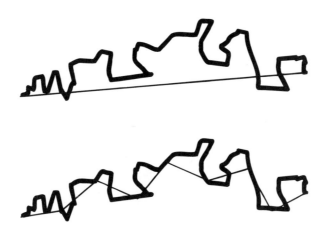

Taking a long step carries you past a lot of tiny indentations (top). Taking shorter steps means that you end up traveling a longer distance along such an indented shoreline (bottom).

This phenomenon in nature illustrates an important property of shapes called *fractals*.

Fractal Geometry

From the meanderings of a pond's edge to the branchings of trees and the intricate forms of snowflakes, shapes in nature are often more complicated than geometrical shapes such as circles, spheres, triangles, cones, rectangles, and cubes. Smooth curves and regular shapes cannot fully describe the complex form of a cloud, a mountain, a leaf, or a coastline.

A close examination of many natural forms reveals that their irregularity has a pattern. Nature is full of shapes that repeat themselves on different scales within the same object.

The curving patterns along each inlet approximate the curves along the entire coastline. A fragment of rock resembles the shape of the mountain from which it broke off. A tree's twigs have the same branching pattern seen near its trunk. The shape of a fern's leaflets may resemble the pattern formed by leaflets on each blade and the pattern formed by blades on each frond of the fern.

Fluffy clouds, jagged rocks, indented shorelines, and bare trees form fractal-like shapes.

Benoit B. Mandelbrot, a mathematics professor at Yale University and an IBM Fellow, was the first person to recognize how amazingly common this type of structure is in nature. In 1975, he coined the term **fractal** for shapes that repeat themselves within an object. The word "fractal" comes from the Latin term for "broken."

Benoit B. Mandelbrot coined the word *fractal* to describe shapes that repeat themselves within an object on smaller scales.

The mathematics of fractals is based on the relationship between patterns in an object and patterns found in parts of the object. In a fractal object, each smaller structure is a miniature, though not necessarily identical, version of the larger form.

Fractal Snowflakes

In 1904, long before Mandelbrot conceived of fractals, Swedish mathematician Helge von Koch created an intriguing but puzzling curve. It zigzags in such an odd pattern that it seems impossible to start at one point and follow the curve to reach another point.

Like many figures now known to be fractals, Koch's curve is easy to generate by starting with a simple figure and turning it into an increasingly crinkly form.

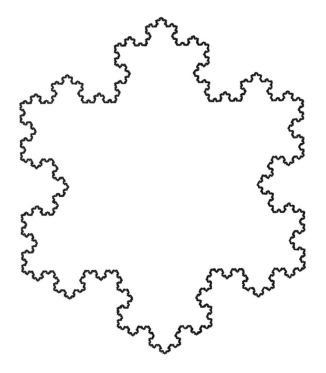

The extremely crinkly boundary of this shape is known as the Koch, or snowflake, curve.

YOU WILL NEED

- pencil
- ruler
- sheet of paper
- protractor for measuring angles to draw triangles

WHAT TO DO

1. Draw an equilateral triangle with each side measuring 9 centimeters. (Remember, each angle of an equilateral triangle measures 60°.)

2. Divide each 9-centimeter side into three parts, each measuring 3 centimeters. At the middle of each side, add an equilateral triangle one third the size of the original, facing outward.

   Because each side of the original triangle is 9 centimeters, the new triangles will have 3-centimeter sides.

   When you examine the outer edge of your diagram you should see a six-pointed star made up of 12 line segments.

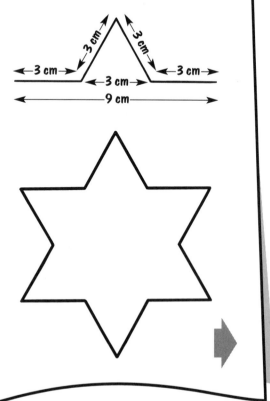

3. At the middle of each segment of the star, add a triangle one ninth the size of the original triangle. The new triangles will have sides 1 centimeter in length, so divide each 3-centimeter segment into thirds, and use the middle third to form a new triangle.

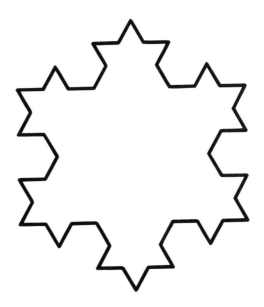

4. Going one step farther, you create a shape that begins to resemble a snowflake.

If you were to continue the process by endlessly adding smaller and smaller triangles to every new side, you would produce the Koch snowflake curve. Between any two points, the snowflake would have an infinite number of zigzags.

So, if an infinitely small ant were racing around a Koch snowflake, its trip would be infinitely long. It is possible to prove that the snowflake's perimeter is infinite, but the area inside it clearly is not!

For more about the Koch snowflake's amazing properties, turn to the last section in this chapter, "Snowflake Perimeters."

Fractal Fun

Drawing fractals can be tedious work, but there are several computer programs available that make it easy to generate fractals. Here's how you can generate a simple tree step by step.

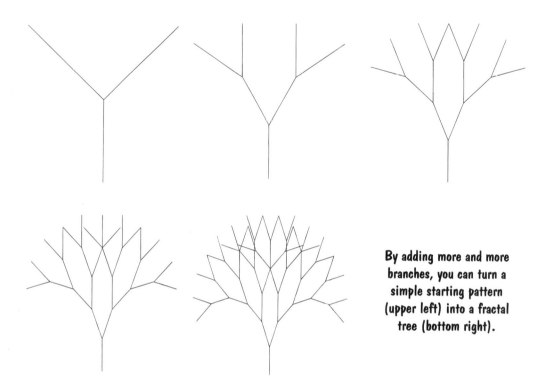

By adding more and more branches, you can turn a simple starting pattern (upper left) into a fractal tree (bottom right).

You can even use computer software to create fractal drawings that resemble real plants and natural landscapes.

Computer programs allow you to produce a variety of fractal patterns that resemble natural objects, such as ferns, trees, and other leafy plants.

Can you figure out what basic shapes and simple rules for going from one step to the next went into the creation of the following computer-generated fractal shapes?

[Answers on p. 101.]

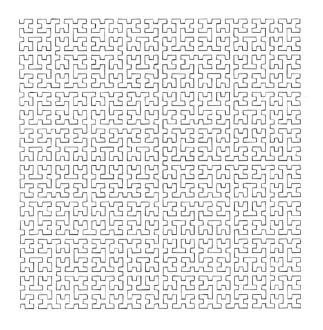

The Hilbert curve (top) and the Sierpinski triangle (bottom) are two famous fractal patterns. Can you figure out the starting patterns and the procedures for creating these shapes?

Mandelbrot's Snowman

The awesome snowman who officiates at the Fractal Pond races is himself a fractal, called the **Mandelbrot set.** This strange, solitary figure is a source of unending wonder among mathematicians.

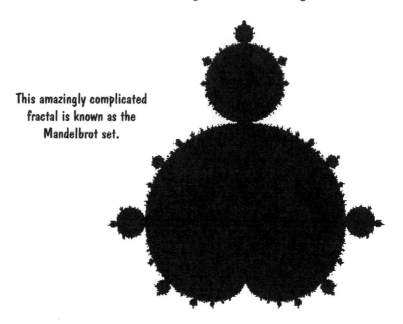

This amazingly complicated fractal is known as the Mandelbrot set.

Close-ups of the border of the Mandelbrot set unveil a riot of fantastic tendrils and complex curlicues.

A close-up of the Mandelbrot set's boundary reveals intricate details.

SNOWFLAKE PERIMETERS

Computing the perimeter of each step in creating a Koch snowflake (see page 46) shows some interesting patterns.

- If the original triangle has 9-centimeter sides, its perimeter is 27 centimeters.

- In Step 2, you produced a star made of 12 segments. If each segment is 3 centimeters, what is the perimeter of the star? Compare your total to the perimeter of the original triangle. You will find that the star's outer edge is four thirds the original triangle's perimeter.

- The third shape has 48 sides, measuring 1 centimeter each. Therefore, its perimeter is 48 centimeters, which is 48/36, or 4/3, the perimeter of the star. If you keep going, you would find out that each step of the Koch snowflake has a perimeter 4/3 that of the perimeter before it.

- The third shape's perimeter of 48 centimeters is 48/27 times the perimeter of the original triangle, and $48/27 = 16/9 = 4^2/3^2$. The fourth shape's perimeter is 64/27, or $4^3/3^3$, that of the original triangle. If this pattern continues, what will be the perimeter of the pattern after 10 steps?

[Answer on p. 102.]

Tilt-A-Whirl Madness

Enough spectating! Tired of watching the poor little ant race along every nook and cranny of Fractal Pond, you feel ready for some wild fun. But where's the action?

From off in the distance, you can make out the sound of kids screaming excitedly. Then the screaming stops. The screams start up again, just briefly, then stop.

J. WOLK-STANLEY '99

The off-and-on screams continue, but they don't seem to follow any pattern. At times, you can hear a whole crowd screaming; at other times, it sounds like just one or two voices. Sometimes the excited shouts continue for a while; sometimes they die down after a second or two. There may be only an instant of silence between screams, or it may stay quiet for so long that you wonder if the wild cries have stopped for good.

The nearest ride you can find on your MathZone map is the Tilt-A-Whirl, so you head toward it in your quest for thrills. As you draw closer, the off-and-on screams grow louder.

You come to a crazily spinning ride. Kids are sitting in seven round cars. Each car is at the edge of its own circular platform, free to spin around on the platform, like the hands moving around the face of a clock.

The seven platforms are traveling at a steady speed along a circular track with three hills and valleys. As the platforms go around the track in a perfectly regular pattern, each car whirls around its platform unpredictably, like a bunch of clocks gone haywire.

Sometimes the cars spin clockwise, sometimes counterclockwise, and sometimes they stop for a moment. You can't possibly predict what will happen next. There's no pattern at all. Each car seems to do its own thing.

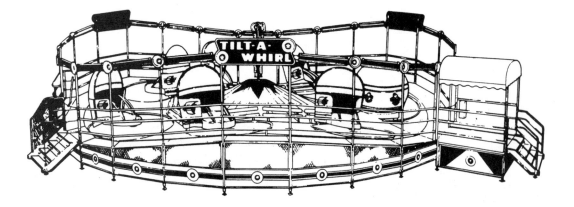

The Tilt-A-Whirl makes wild, unpredictable movements.

"You're next!" says a man, pointing straight at you. He is wearing a cowboy hat and a shirt covered with swirling tornadoes.

When the Tilt-A-Whirl stops and unloads its laughing, screaming riders, you run to the first empty car and climb in. You take a deep breath. Soon all the cars are filled with eager riders, and the platforms start to move innocently along the track.

As your car speeds up, you suddenly whiz around to the left! Before you can catch your breath, you whirl to the right. You hold on tight for a trip back to the left, but your car hesitates and goes nowhere. Then *BAM!* You find yourself spinning to the right again, then back the other way—and then left some more.

It's total chaos. You are whirling out of control and screaming with excitement. Your mind is jangling. Your stomach is churning. You have no idea what to expect.

After a few minutes, the platforms start to slow down and your car stops twirling. As you go over the next hill, your car turns once around to the right. It keeps on making one twirl with each hill, very predictably. There are no more unexpected turns.

"Faster, faster!" the riders demand.

"Okay, folks, time to rev it up," calls the man in the tornado shirt.

Feeling your platform start to move faster than ever along the track, you hold on tight for the biggest thrill yet. Each car swings to the outer edge of its platform, but nobody spins. The platforms just go up and down along the track, as if this were just a carousel ride with little hills. Boring, boring!

What could bring back the thrills?

[Answer follows.]

Mathematical Chaos

Mathematicians studying the Tilt-A-Whirl have found that when the platforms travel at very low speeds along the track, the cars complete one backward revolution each time their platforms go over a hill. At high speeds, each car swings to its platform's outer edge and stays locked in that position.

But at intermediate speeds—around 6.5 revolutions per minute— the cars move in chaotic, unpredictable ways. To bring back the excitement, the operator will need to slow down the Tilt-A-Whirl to roughly that speed.

How much you weigh and where you sit on the car seat also affect your car's movements. The Tilt-A-Whirl's jumbled mixture of rotations and spins never repeats itself exactly. That's what makes the ride a thrilling, unpredictable experience. No two trips are ever likely to produce quite the same thrills and chills.

The Tilt-A-Whirl illustrates a phenomenon called **chaos.** Chaos occurs when systems governed by physical laws undergo transitions to a highly irregular form of behavior. Although chaotic movements appear random, they are actually governed by strict mathematical conditions. For the Tilt-A-Whirl, speed is one of those conditions.

Chaos arises in many settings. For example, it can appear in the irregular dripping pattern of a leaky faucet, in stock-market price fluctuations, and in the tiny variations of a person's heartbeat. Even something as simple as a pendulum hanging from another pendulum can move chaotically.

Double Trouble

The double pendulum is a simple physical system that can readily shift from an apparently orderly, predictable motion to the erratic, unpredictable motion of a chaotic system.

A single pendulum consists of a weight hanging from a string or a rod pivoted at one end. It swings back and forth. In a double pendulum, a second rod is added, which pivots from the bottom of the first rod. Adding the second rod greatly increases the motion's complexity.

In a double pendulum, a second pendulum is suspended below the first pendulum, greatly complicating the possible movements.

Here's a chaos machine that you can build.

- - - - - - - - - -

YOU WILL NEED

- some string

- two drinking straws, one long and one short (about one third as long)

- two balls of clay or other small weights (fishing sinkers work well)

- - - - - - - - - -

WHAT TO DO

1. Tie a piece of string around a ball of clay. Thread the string through the long straw, pulling it tight so that the clay ball is jammed against the straw's end. Attach the other end of the string to the edge of a table so that the pendulum can swing freely. Let it swing.

2. Tie a piece of string around another ball of clay. Thread the string through the short straw, again pulling the ball tightly against the straw's end. This time, tie the free end of the string to the clay ball at the bottom of the pendulum you made in Step 1, making a double pendulum.

3. Make sure you have enough room, then set the double pendulum swinging. Try different starting positions. What do you find when you start the swing at small angles? Large angles? When is the motion regular? Unpredictable?

[Answer on p. 102.]

The double pendulum swings unpredictably. Sometimes it moves in wide arcs; at other times, it sways just briefly; and sometimes it pauses before resuming its chaotic course. At times, the lower rod does all the swinging, while at other times, the upper rod carries the bulk of the motion. There are even times when a double pendulum acts as if it were a single pendulum.

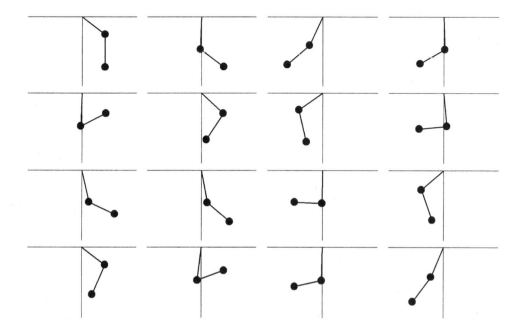

Just a few of the possible chaotic movements of a double pendulum are shown here.

Like all chaotic systems, a double pendulum's movements tend to change drastically in response to slight changes in initial conditions. If you had two double pendulums starting at slightly different positions, their movements would differ dramatically.

You can explore chaos with numbers, too. Try this experiment.

YOU WILL NEED

- calculator

WHAT TO DO

1. Pick a one-digit decimal number between 0 and 1 (such as 0.2 or 0.7) as your starting number.

2. Enter the number 1 into your calculator.

3. Subtract your starting number from 1.

4. Multiply the answer from Step 3 by your starting number.

5. Multiply the answer from Step 4 by 4.

6. Use the answer from Step 5 as your next starting number, and repeat Steps 2 through 6. For example,

   Start with 0.2.

   Enter 1.

   Subtract your starting number:

   $1 - 0.2 = 0.8$

   Multiply by your starting number:

   $0.8 \times 0.2 = 0.16$

   Multiply by 4:

   $0.16 \times 4 = 0.64$

If you start with 0.64 and repeat Steps 2 though 5, you will end up with 0.922.

If you keep on using your answer to repeat the process eight times, you get this set of numbers (rounded to three decimal places): 0.2, 0.64, 0.922, 0.289, 0.822, 0.586, 0.970, 0.116, 0.406.

7. Now start with a number that just slightly differs from your original number. In the example, the original number is 0.2, so this time you might pick 0.21. After going through Steps 2 though 5, you get 0.664. Repeat the process eight times, and you get these numbers (rounded to three decimal places): 0.21, 0.664, 0.892, 0.364, 0.926, 0.275, 0.796, 0.650, 0.910.

8. Compare the two sets of answers:

> Starting with 0.20
> 0.64, 0.922, 0.289, 0.822, 0.586, 0.97, 0.116, 0.406
>
> Starting with 0.21
> 0.664, 0.892, 0.364, 0.926, 0.275, 0.796, 0.650, 0.910

The second starting number is only a bit different from the first, but the more times you perform each set of calculations, the more the answers diverge. That's a key feature of chaos.

9. Try other starting numbers (maybe even a slightly different formula) to see what happens. You'll find all sorts of surprises.

HISTORY OF THE TILT-A-WHIRL

The Tilt-A-Whirl first operated in 1926 at an amusement park in White Bear Lake, Minnesota. The ride's inventor, Herbert W. Sellner, probably discovered its unpredictable movements not through mathematical analysis but by building the machine and trying it out.

Tilt-A-Whirl riders enjoy Herbert Sellner's invention.

"Ride designers have been fairly adept at finding chaos without appreciating the mathematical underpinning of what they're doing," says Richard L. Kautz, a physicist at the National Institute of Standards and Technology. Kautz and Bret M. Huggard, a physicist at Northern Arizona University, have analyzed the Tilt-A-Whirl's motions, and they believe that several other amusement park rides also move in a way that is mathematically chaotic.

In fact, ride manufacturers are now beginning to use mathematical analyses and computer simulations to help build chaotic motion into new amusement park rides to create thrills that are more exciting than ever!

Luck on the Boredwalk

"Shoot the prime number!" "Make a whole-in-one!" "Throw a pi at the highest face value!" As you wander along the busy Boredwalk at the edge of the MathZone, it's hard to decide which game to try first.

"Come play a game of Piggy!" calls out a girl standing behind a booth framed with photos of fat little pigs.

Jessica Wolk-Stanley '99

Wondering what Piggy is, you saunter over. You notice little horseshoes dangling from the girl's earrings. She sets two pairs of dice on the counter.

"Here's how to play," she explains. "We each take a pair of dice. When it's your turn, you roll your dice, and your score is the face value of the dice. So if you roll a three and a four, you get seven points. The first player to get 100 points wins. You keep on rolling as many times as you want in a turn, but if you roll doubles, you lose all the points you have accumulated in that turn, and your turn is over. You try to stay with a turn long enough to get lots of points."

"But don't get 'piggy' about it," she warns. "If you roll too many times, you will eventually get doubles and lose all your points."

"Which pair of dice will you choose?" the girl asks.

You study the dice suspiciously. One pair looks perfectly normal. Each die has six faces, and each face is labeled 1, 2, 3, 4, 5, or 6, in the ordinary fashion:

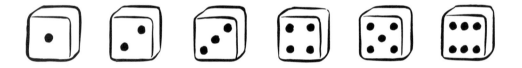

The other pair of dice, however, has faces labeled 1, 2, 2, 3, 3, and 4 on one die and 1, 3, 4, 5, 6, and 8 on the other.

"Need help deciding?" She takes out a big chart that shows all the possible outcomes from rolling each pair of dice.

Standard Dice	⚀ 1	⚁ 2	⚂ 3	⚃ 4	⚄ 5	⚅ 6
⚀ 1	2	3	4	5	6	7
⚁ 2	3	4	5	6	7	8
⚂ 3	4	5	6	7	8	9
⚃ 4	5	6	7	8	9	10
⚄ 5	6	7	8	9	10	11
⚅ 6	7	8	9	10	11	12

Weird Dice	1	2	2	3	3	4
1	2	3	3	4	4	5
3	4	5	5	6	6	7
4	5	6	6	7	7	8
5	6	7	7	8	8	9
6	7	8	8	9	9	10
8	9	10	10	11	11	12

"Your chances of rolling any particular number are the same with either pair of dice," she explains. "See? The chart shows that there is only one way to roll a sum of two with the standard dice. Same for the weird dice. There are two ways to roll a sum of three using either pair of dice."

Studying the chart, you see that both sets of dice have three possible combinations that add up to 4, four possible 5s, five possible 6s, six possible 7s, five combinations that total 8, four 9s, three 10s, two 11s, and one 12.

Should you play it safe and use the standard dice or try the weird pair?

[Answer on p. 102.]

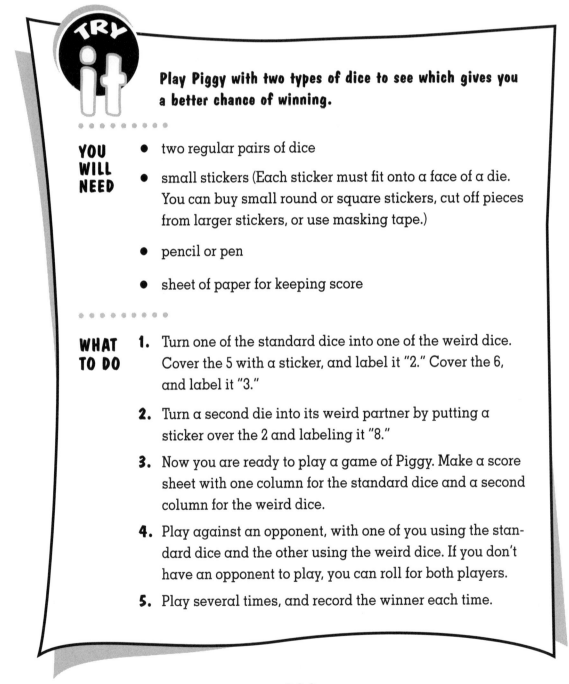

Play Piggy with two types of dice to see which gives you a better chance of winning.

YOU WILL NEED

- two regular pairs of dice
- small stickers (Each sticker must fit onto a face of a die. You can buy small round or square stickers, cut off pieces from larger stickers, or use masking tape.)
- pencil or pen
- sheet of paper for keeping score

WHAT TO DO

1. Turn one of the standard dice into one of the weird dice. Cover the 5 with a sticker, and label it "2." Cover the 6, and label it "3."

2. Turn a second die into its weird partner by putting a sticker over the 2 and labeling it "8."

3. Now you are ready to play a game of Piggy. Make a score sheet with one column for the standard dice and a second column for the weird dice.

4. Play against an opponent, with one of you using the standard dice and the other using the weird dice. If you don't have an opponent to play, you can roll for both players.

5. Play several times, and record the winner each time.

Weird Dice

If you have constructed the weird dice so that all sides have an equal chance of coming up, the player rolling the weird dice will usually win. Can you figure out why?

Here's a hint: Study the chart on page 65 showing sums for each pair of dice. How many ways are there to roll a double with the standard dice? How many with the weird dice?

[Answer on p. 102.]

Remember, the "piggy" player who rolls doubles most often usually loses.

Playing Monopoly with Weird Dice

Changing the dice can make a big difference in many board games in which rolling doubles or other special combinations affects a player's fate. If you have the game Monopoly, you can try playing it with the weird dice from the MathZone Piggy game and see whether that changes the game.

Many mathematicians have studied the probabilities involved in this classic board game in which players buy, sell, rent, and trade real estate in a cutthroat competition to bankrupt their opponents. Players take turns throwing a pair of dice to determine how many spaces to proceed along the track, which consists of 22 real estate properties, 4 railroads, 2 utilities, 1 jail, and 11 other squares. Rolling doubles gives you an extra turn, but rolling doubles three times in a row sends you to jail.

Mathematical studies have shown that Monopoly players are likely to spend much more time in jail or visiting jail than on any other square in the game. To get out of jail, a player has to pay $50 or roll doubles.

Might using the weird dice change your strategy?

[Answer on p. 102.]

Here is an experiment you can perform to see how playing with the weird dice affects Monopoly when players try to get out of jail by rolling doubles.

YOU WILL NEED
- traditional edition of the game Monopoly
- pair of standard dice
- pair of weird dice (see page 66)

WHAT TO DO

1. Stack the Chance cards face down on the board.

2. Set out the deeds for the following properties: Electric Company, Virginia Avenue, St. James Place, and Tennessee Avenue.

3. Pretend you are in the middle of a game in which two players are both stuck in jail. Give each player $50 and place two playing pieces on the jail square.

4. Give each player a different pair of dice. Player 1 uses only the standard dice, and player 2 uses only the weird dice.

HOW TO PLAY

1. Take turns rolling the dice. When a player rolls doubles, move the piece the corresponding number of spaces from jail.

2. Pretend there is a third player who owns the Electric Company (2 spaces from jail), Virginia Avenue (4 spaces), St. James Place (6 spaces), and Tennessee Avenue (8 spaces). When you roll doubles and land on one of those squares, you must pay the "Rent" amount shown on each property deed: $12 for Virginia Avenue; $14 for St. James Place; and $14 for Tennessee Avenue.

Landing on the Electric Company costs $8 because you pay four times the number rolled. (The Electric Company is 2 spaces from jail, and 4 × 2 = 8.) A player who rolls double 5s lands on "Free Parking" and pays nothing. Rolling double 6s takes you to Chance. Draw a Chance card and do what it says.

3. After paying rent, return to jail for your next turn and continue trying to roll doubles.

4. When one player runs out of money, the other player wins.

Which pair of dice do you think is more likely to produce a winner?

If you repeat the experiment enough times, you will probably find that the player using the weird dice lands on St. James Place more often than anywhere else. That's because St. James Place is six spaces away from jail. There are two ways to roll a double 3 with the weird dice, but there's only one way to roll other doubles using the regular dice or the weird dice.

ANALYZING MONOPOLY

In the early 1980s, two students at the University of Minnesota—Duluth calculated how playing Monopoly with the weird dice increases the value of some properties and decreases the value of others. For example, it increases the value of St. James Place because the owner is likely to collect lots of rent from players leaving jail.

On the other hand, playing Monopoly with the weird dice decreases the chances of landing on Virginia Avenue, which is four spaces from jail. It is impossible to roll a double 2 with the weird dice.

It's fun to experiment with different ways of numbering dice to see how the numbering can change various games of chance. One amazing set of four dice lets you win like magic every time! Try this mind-boggling dice game for two players.

YOU WILL NEED

- two pairs of standard dice
- small stickers
- pen or pencil
- sheet of paper for keeping score

WHAT TO DO

Relabel the four dice by placing stickers on each face and marking them as follows:

First die: 0, 0, 4, 4, 4, 4

Second die: 3, 3, 3, 3, 3, 3

Third die: 2, 2, 2, 2, 6, 6

Fourth die: 1, 1, 1, 5, 5, 5

HOW TO PLAY

1. Let your opponent pick any one of the four dice.

2. You choose one of the remaining three. Use this secret strategy:

   If your opponent chooses the die with the 4s, you choose the one with the 5s.

   If your opponent chooses the die with the 3s, you choose the one with the 4s.

   If your opponent chooses the die with the 2s, you choose the one with the 3s.

   If your opponent chooses the die with the 5s, you choose the one with the 6s.

3. Each player tosses his or her die, and the highest number wins the throw.

4. Keep a tally of who wins each throw.

5. After 10 or 20 throws, you will probably be the winner.

6. Invite your opponent to choose another die, even the one you were using.

7. Again, if you choose the right die, you are very likely to win after 10 or more throws.

Bradley Efron, a statistician at Stanford University, designed this game to show a paradox: If A beats B, and B beats C, then one would usually assume that A beats C. Not with these dice! The special way in which they are numbered means that no matter which die your opponent chooses, you can pick a die that will beat it most of the time.

The Code-Locked Door

Lions, tigers, and bears? Elephants and alligators? The building ahead of you has wild animals painted all over it! Is this the MathZone zoo, or what?

You come to a door covered with a leopard-skin print. You try to enter, but the door is locked. You knock. No answer.

DECODE TO ENTER

WILD GAME
HALL

Jessica Wolk-Stanley '99

Staring at the leopard skin, you notice that a few of the leopard's spots are regular geometric shapes. One spot is circular; another is rectangular. There's a spot shaped like an oval (or ellipse) and one like a football stadium.

The leopard-skin print on the door to the Wild Game Hall has spots of various shapes.

You see a sign tacked onto the door. It says "Decode to Enter," followed by a bunch of ones and zeros.

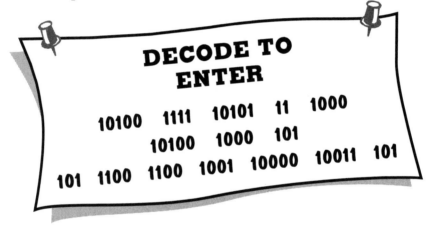

DECODE TO ENTER

10100   1111   10101   11   1000
10100   1000   101
101   1100   1100   1001   10000   10011   101

Can you crack the code to get inside?

[Answer on p. 102.]

Base Two

The ones and zeros you see in the message look like numbers in base two. That's the type of numbering system used in computers.

When a tiny electrical circuit inside a computer is on, it represents a one. When it's off, that's a zero. A computer has millions of circuits that turn on and off in different combinations. To make a computer do anything, you need a way to express numbers, letters, and other symbols using "on" and "off," or "1" and "0." You need a numbering system that has only two digits.

Our regular base-ten numbering system uses ten digits: 1, 2, 3, 4, 5, 6, 7, 8, 9, and 0. In the number 5,280, the 0 is in the ones column, 8 is in the tens column, 2 is in the hundreds column, and 5 is in the thousands column.

A base two, or **binary,** numbering system has only two digits: 0 and 1. In place of the ones, tens, hundreds, and thousands columns (representing powers of ten), the columns represent powers of two. The right-hand digit is in the ones column, the next digit is in the 2s column, then 4s, 8s, 16s, 32s, and so on.

Number Quirks

Here are the first ten numbers, expressed in three different numbering systems.

Roman Numeral	Base Ten		Base Two (Binary)			
(No place-value columns)	10s	1s	8s	4s	2s	1s
I		1				1
II		2			1	0
III		3			1	1
IV		4		1	0	0
V		5		1	0	1
VI		6		1	1	0
VII		7		1	1	1
VIII		8	1	0	0	0
IX		9	1	0	0	1
X	1	0	1	0	1	0

Having a **place value** for each column is very useful for adding, multiplying, and performing other calculations. How long does it take you to figure out 243 + 75 in base ten? Now try the same calculation with Roman numerals, which have no place values: CCXLIII + LXXV.

Many calculations in modern mathematics are easier to perform in base two, using a computer, than to perform in base ten. For example, mathematicians use computers to search for Mersenne primes in base two, partly because a Mersenne number consists entirely of a string of a certain number of ones (see Trek 5). For instance, the Mersenne number 7 can be expressed as the binary number 111, and 31 as 11111.

Binary digits are also handy for communicating messages reliably and accurately from place to place over a computer network or via cell phones, and for reproducing sound digitally, such as the music you get from a compact disc.

TRY it

To decode the message on the door, try converting each base-two numeral to base ten. To do that, add together the place values of each base-two digit.

Here's the first line:

$$10100 = 16 + 0 + 4 + 0 + 0 = 20$$

$$1111 = 8 + 4 + 2 + 1 = 15$$

$$10101 = 16 + 0 + 4 + 0 + 1 = 21$$

$$11 = 2 + 1 = 3$$

$$1000 = 8 + 0 + 0 + 0 = 8$$

In base ten, the first word would be 20-15-21-3-8.

Often, in a coded message, each number represents a letter of the alphabet. Can you figure out what the coded word is if 1 = A, 2 = B, 3 = C, and so on?

[Answer on p. 102.]

Because T is the twentieth letter of the alphabet, the first number— 20—represents the letter T. The second number—15—represents the letter O. See whether you can figure out the rest of the word.

Once you have the letters for 20-15-21-3-8, you are ready to decode the entire message and find out how to open the door!

This table may help you decode the message.

1 = A	7 = G	13 = M	19 = S	25 = Y
2 = B	8 = H	14 = N	20 = T	26 = Z
3 = C	9 = I	15 = O	21 = U	
4 = D	10 = J	16 = P	22 = V	
5 = E	11 = K	17 = Q	23 = W	
6 = F	12 = L	18 = R	24 = X	

How Spies Send Messages

What if you were a spy and you wanted to send a top-secret e-mail message to your boss?

If you used a simple code in which each number stands for a certain letter of the alphabet, it wouldn't be very difficult for an enemy to intercept your e-mail and decipher your message—just as you deciphered the message on the Wild Game Hall door. The enemy would try different possible letter substitutions and look for patterns.

Modern spies use special mathematical formulas to keep their computer messages secret. In a computer, each letter of the alphabet is assigned a number. Inside a computer, the base-two number 010000001 represents the letter A. The number 010000010 stands for B; the letter C is 010000011, and so on.

Can you figure out the letter Z? Because Z is the twenty-sixth letter of the English alphabet, convert 26 to base two: That's $16 + 8 + 0 + 2 + 0$, or 11010. Then put 010 in front of the number, and you get $Z = 01011010$.

Using a mathematical formula called a "key," the computer scrambles the numbers of the original message so much that no outsider can possibly decipher it, even by trying billions and billions of possible answers. The only way to understand the message is to use a computer programmed with the proper mathematical key for deciphering the words.

Everyday Secrecy

Spies aren't the only ones who use mathematical formulas to create covert e-mail messages. Banks conceal money information sent from one computer to another so that no outsider can find out how much money is in a customer's account. Businesses hide their plans for selling new products so that competing companies can't copy them. Military leaders share secret strategies for defending their country against foreign attack.

Suppose your secret message is "HELP." You can hide it with a mathematical lock and key.

YOU WILL NEED

- sheet of paper
- pencil

WHAT TO DO

1. First translate HELP into computer code. Because H = 8, E = 5, L = 12, and P = 16, the base-two code for HELP is 01001000-01000101-01001100-01010000.

2. Create a "key" that has the same number of digits as the message. The key, in this case, would consist of 32 ones and zeros, chosen randomly. One way to come up with random digits is to roll a die 32 times. Write "0" each time you roll an even number. Write "1" each time an odd number comes up. Write the secret key under the message, with the digits lined up.

Message	01001000	01000101	01001100	01010000
Secret Key	10100010	10101010	10100101	01110101

3. Add the two sets of numbers column by column, using these special addition rules: 0 + 0 = 0, 0 + 1 = 1, 1 + 0 = 1, and 1 + 1 = 0. The result will be your coded message.

Message	01001000	01000101	01001100	01010000
Secret Key	10100010	10101010	10100101	01110101
Coded Message	11101010	11101111	11101001	00100101

4. Give your secret key to a partner. Also give your partner the coded message. Your partner can figure out your original message by adding the key to the secret message, column by column, following the same addition rules that you used to encode the message.

To see how your partner would decode your message, do the addition to fill in the following blanks.

Coded Message	11101010	11101111	11101001	00100101
Secret Key	10100010	10101010	10100101	01110101
Decoded Message				

[Answer on p. 102.]

· ·

ADA LOVELACE: PROGRAMMER, MATHEMATICIAN

Programming languages, such as BASIC, LOGO, and C++, tell computers how to process millions of 1s and 0s.

In the 1970s, computer programmers designed a new language for the U.S. government's data-processing needs. They named the language Ada, in honor of Ada Byron King, Countess of Lovelace, a nineteenth-century mathematician. The computer language Ada is still used in many of today's computers.

Ada was the daughter of the famous English poet Lord Byron. He left the family when Ada was only a year old, so Ada was raised by her mother Annabella, who loved mathematics.

Because there were no schools for women in England at the time, Annabella hired tutors for her daughter. Ada was unusually good at understanding mathematical concepts and writing about them.

Ada Byron King, Countess of Lovelace, thoroughly enjoyed mathematics and wrote the world's first computer program.

As a young woman, Ada married Lord Lovelace, had a child, and also became deeply involved in mathematics. She ended up working with Charles Babbage, the mathematician who, in the 1830s, designed what amounted to the world's first general-purpose computer.

To make complex calculations faster and more accurate, Babbage designed what he called an "analytical engine." Babbage's idea was to use a series of "program" cards to tell the machine which operations were to be performed (addition, subtraction, multiplication, division, and so on) and in what order. "Data" cards would represent the numbers to be worked with. After some Italian scientists wrote an article about Babbage's ideas, he asked Ada to translate the article from Italian to English.

When the translation was first published, the title page said it was "translated with notes by A. A. L." The customs of the time did not allow a woman to use her full name in a book. Lovelace's "notes" really amounted to a separate paper that included "diagrams" showing the steps needed to instruct the analytical engine to solve certain problems.

Ada had written the first one of what we now call computer programs.

The Wild Game Hall

WARNING:
Attempting to enter this building without following the encoded instructions may be hazardous to your luck.

Having decoded the message on the door (see *Trek 17*), you follow the mysterious instructions. The door smoothly swings open. You step into a quiet room lined with leather chairs and card tables. There is no one in sight, but you hear loud knocking coming from a doorway. It sounds like deer banging their antlers together in battle, or maybe bowling balls crashing into pins.

Jessica Wolk-Stanley '99

As you step through the doorway, the irregular knocking grows louder, and you enter a big, noisy, dimly lit room full of tables. Some kids are playing air hockey, and others are throwing darts. A few more are standing in front of tables that are propped up on one side to create a slope.

On the nearest table, you can see an array of long, thin nails stuck upright into its surface to form a sort of geometric pincushion. A player pulls back a shooter, sending a metal ball to the top of the array. The ball bounces off the pins in a random motion, gradually making its way down the slope. Each collision between ball and pin generates an amplified clang. It looks like an old-fashioned pinball game!

Wandering on, you come to several tables covered with the familiar green felt found on billiard tables. A cone of bright light illuminates each surface.

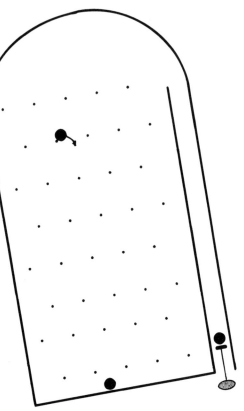

In this simple pinball game, a player sends a ball to the top of an array of metal pins stuck upright in a tilted board, then watches the ball bounce off the pins randomly as it falls down the slope.

The players gathered around the tables all hold long, tapered sticks. Occasionally, they lean over and squint at the gleaming balls scattered across each green surface. The tables have six pockets along their rims, into which balls can fall.

You watch a player adjust her stance and lower her billiard cue, aiming the tip directly at one of the balls. A smooth stroke ending in a sharp tap shoots the ball across the surface. The ball bounces off one cushion, then another, before knocking squarely into a second ball.

You wonder what version of billiards, or pool, they are playing.
Then you notice a dusty old poster hanging on the wall.

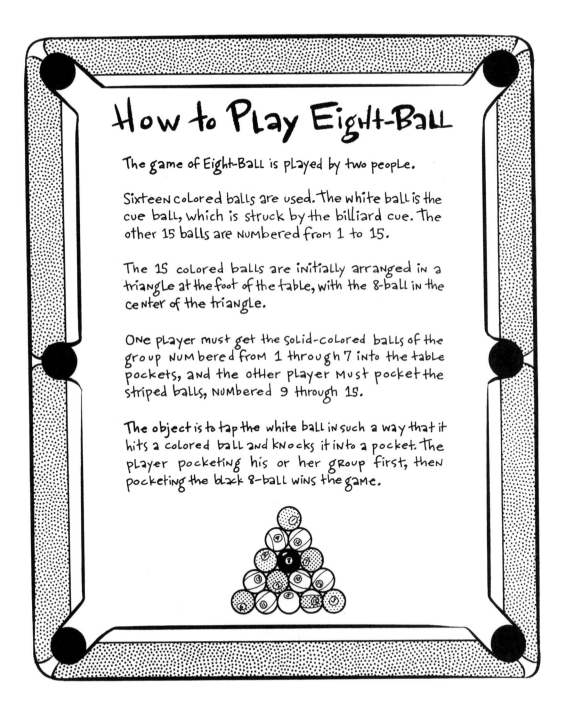

How to Play Eight-Ball

The game of Eight-Ball is played by two people.

Sixteen colored balls are used. The white ball is the cue ball, which is struck by the billiard cue. The other 15 balls are numbered from 1 to 15.

The 15 colored balls are initially arranged in a triangle at the foot of the table, with the 8-ball in the center of the triangle.

One player must get the solid-colored balls of the group numbered from 1 through 7 into the table pockets, and the other player must pocket the striped balls, numbered 9 through 15.

The object is to tap the white ball in such a way that it hits a colored ball and knocks it into a pocket. The player pocketing his or her group first, then pocketing the black 8-ball wins the game.

What you observe in the Wild Game Hall, however, is clearly not a normal game of eight-ball or pool. For one thing, there are never more than three or four balls on the table.

At the next table over, a little girl in a ponytail, who is barely taller than the table, taps a ball with her cue, not bothering to aim at all. The ball bounces off the edge and smacks directly into a second ball. A perfect hit!

At a third table, a player who looks like a college student carefully examines possible angles before aiming his cue. He shoots with faultless expertise, but the ball ricochets wildly from one side to another, never hitting any other ball.

"I quit!" the player shouts. "This game is rigged. The ball goes crazy every time I hit it. There's no way you can possibly win." He stomps off, and, on his way out the door, he hands the stick to you, murmuring, "YOU try it!"

A boy wearing a leopard-skin vest motions you over. "You may use any of these five tables," he says.

As the players move aside, you study the tables and realize that they are not all rectangular. One has an oval shape called an **ellipse,** another is circular, and a third is rounded at each end, like a football stadium. There are also two normal-looking rectangular tables, but one of them has a wooden ring in the middle.

The billiard tables in the Wild Game Hall have different shapes.

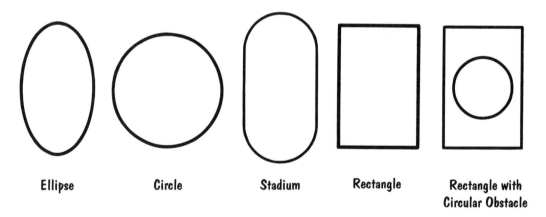

| Ellipse | Circle | Stadium | Rectangle | Rectangle with Circular Obstacle |

Which table would be your best bet to guarantee a hit? (Hint: Remember the coded message.)

[Answer on p. 103.]

Billiards in the Round

The geometrical shape of a billiard table can greatly affect the types of shots possible in a game if the ball has to bounce off the sides several times before hitting another ball. Going from a rectangle to a circle, an oval, or a stadium shape introduces new elements into the game—even chaos and unpredictability.

One mathematician who thought of playing billiards on a circular table was Charles Dodgson, who as Lewis Carroll wrote *Alice's Adventures in Wonderland*. Dodgson also worked on the four-color map problem (—*see Trek 2*).

In 1890, Dodgson published a set of rules for a two-player game of circular billiards. He specified that the circular table must have a cushion all around, no pockets, and a surface marked with three spots in an equilateral triangle.

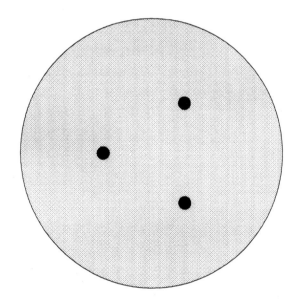

This circular billiard table was designed by Charles Dodgson, whose pen name was Lewis Carroll.

The game begins with three balls of different colors placed on the spots. If the cue ball hits a cushion and then hits a ball, the player scores one point. If the player's cue ball hits two balls, the player scores two points. Hitting a ball, then a cushion, then a ball scores three points; cushion, ball, ball scores four points; and cushion, ball, cushion, ball scores five points.

• • •

You can analyze a ball's motion on a billiard table by imagining the path a ball would follow if it could travel at a constant speed forever, bouncing around from cushion to cushion. At all times, the ball moves in a straight line until it hits a cushion, then it rebounds. When it rebounds, it obeys a basic rule of physics: The angle between the incoming ball's path and the cushion equals the angle between the outgoing ball's path and the cushion.

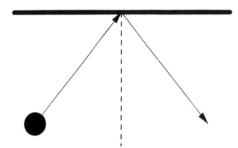

When a ball bounces off a flat surface, the angle between the incoming ball's path and the wall equals the angle between the outgoing ball's path and the wall.

If you had a single billiard ball traveling at a constant speed on a circular table with no pockets, its movements could follow the lines shown in the following diagram. Depending on the ball's starting position and initial direction, it can follow paths that never cross anywhere near the center of the table! So any other ball sitting in that inner region would never get hit.

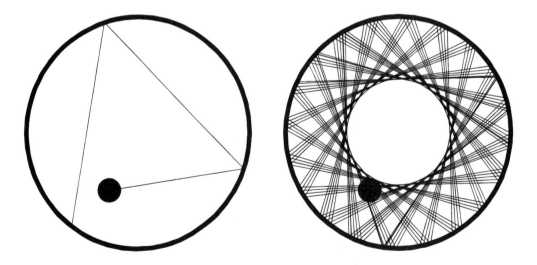

The path of a billiard ball on a circular table after 2 bounces (left) and after about 100 bounces (right) never enters the center of the table.

If you have access to a rectangular pool table or an air-hockey table, try setting a large circular pan, hoop, or other round object in the center. Put a weight on the object to keep it in place, then see how the curved obstacle affects the movements of the balls or the hockey puck.

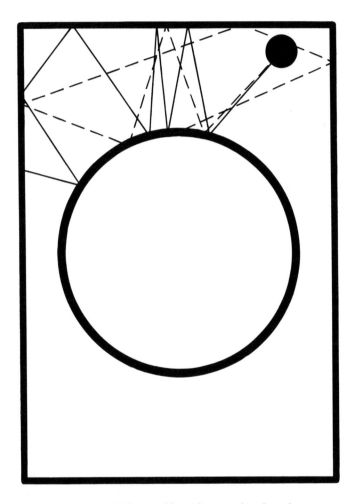

On a rectangular billiard table with a circular obstacle, just a slight change in the initial direction of the ball produces a strikingly different path after several bounces. A ball following the dashed line ends up far away from a ball following the solid line.

Balls or pucks that start off in slightly different directions will follow paths that diverge rapidly with each bounce. Such chaotic movements also occur on a stadium-shaped table.

What would happen on an elliptical table?

[Answer follows.]

Here's how you can draw an ellipse. As you draw, you will get some clues about what sorts of paths to expect on an elliptical billiard table.

· · · · · · · · · ·

YOU WILL NEED

- pencil
- sheet of paper
- two pins or thumbtacks
- piece of string about 10 inches (25 cm) long
- cardboard or another hard, flat surface into which you can stick the pins

· · · · · · · · · ·

WHAT TO DO

1. Tie one end of the string to one of the pins and the other end to the other pin.

2. Place the paper on cardboard or similar drawing surface and stick in the two pins so that they are about 6 inches (15 cm) apart.

3. Using the point of a pencil to keep the string taut, allow the pencil to trace a path around the pins.

Your pencil traces out an ellipse. The locations of the two pins represent the ellipse's two **focal points.** The focal points are positioned so that the distance from one focal point to any point on the curve and then over to the other focal point is always the same.

Think of your ellipse as a billiard table with a ball sitting at each of the two pinpoints. The string shows the path that either of the balls can take when hit. No matter which direction you hit the ball, it will bounce off the edge and head directly to the other ball.

Success in Billiards

Remember the little girl who could hit a ball without aiming?

An elliptical billiard table and properly placed balls were probably the secret of her success. If two balls on an elliptical billiard table sit on the ellipse's two focal points, you can shoot one of the balls in any direction, and it will hit the edge, bounce off, and collide with the other ball.

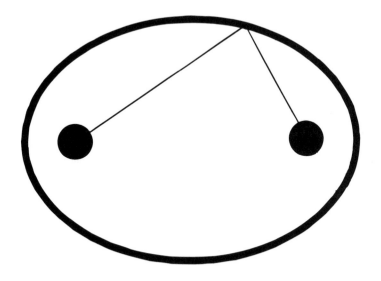

On a billiard table shaped like an ellipse, a ball on one of
the ellipse's focal points, shot in any direction, will always
hit a ball placed on the ellipse's other focal point.

THE CHAOTIC PINBALL MACHINE

A rectangular billiard table studded with round obstacles, or bumpers, produces the same kind of unpredictability as a stadium-shaped table with rounded ends. If you tried to duplicate a shot, you would find that the second ball takes a very different path from the first. Each bounce of the ball off a bumper makes the second ball's path even more different from the first ball's path.

A pinball machine takes advantage of such uncertainty to add elements of suspense and surprise. Today's electronic pinball machines are full of flashing lights, sound effects, fancy bumpers, and flippers. The original pinball machine, however, was simply a sloping surface with an array of pins.

A player would insert a coin, pull back a spring-loaded shooter, fire a metal ball to the top of the array, then watch the ball roll down the slope. Each time the ball struck a pin, its path would change, sometimes going to one side, sometimes to the other side, and eventually ending up at the bottom.

In the 1930s, such pinball machines were often installed in drugstores and restaurants. In his book *The Essence of Chaos*, meteorologist Edward N. Lorenz describes how the machines affected students at Dartmouth College when he was a student there.

"Soon many students were occasionally winning, but more often losing, considerable numbers of nickels," he writes. "Before long the town authorities decided that the machines violated the gambling laws and would have to be removed, but they were eventually persuaded, temporarily at least, that the machines were contests of skill rather than games of chance, and were therefore perfectly legal."

We now know that when physical laws involve the phenomenon called chaos, it is hard to separate skill from luck. The flippers in modern pinball machines add an element of skill to a game that is otherwise mostly random.

Way Out!

A red neon sign glows above the doorway at the back of the Wild Game Hall.

In search of your next adventure, you wander over and exit through the door.

Stepping outside, you blink in the blindingly bright sunshine. As your eyes adjust, you realize you are standing at the top of a giant slide. The slide is studded with soft, leathery obstacles, which look like pillowy punching bags.

"Watch me go!" calls out a boy wearing a Tarzan outfit. He slides down and smacks into one of the giant punching bags, then bounces off to the left, screaming "Yahooooooo!"

Continuing downward, he careens into another bumper and bounces off again. Like a human pinball, he keeps sliding and bouncing erratically from side to side, all the way to the bottom.

With cushioned walls blocking the way on both sides, you realize your only way out is down the wild slide. Gritting your teeth, you zoom toward the first bumper. The soft, springy punching bag shoves you over to the right—without hurting you at all.

Before you can figure out where you are, you spring off another bumper. Surprise! You bounce upward, nearly all the way to the top, then slide swiftly through an open, bumper-free zone. You wonder where you could possibly end up next.

Bam! Your left arm hammers a bumper. The collision sends you spinning around into another bumper, then up and over to another, filling your brain with the same chaotic craziness that drove you wild on the Tilt-A-Whirl.

Finally reaching the bottom, you catch your breath and gaze at a picket fence ahead, with a sign on the gate.

Fractal Maze 1
Find the Way Out!

The picket fence turns in different directions, forming a small maze. You study its pattern from where you are standing.

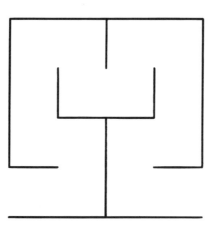

**Fractal Maze 1 is
fairly simple.**

You go through the gate and easily find your way to the "WAY OUT!" sign. As soon as you leave Maze 1, however, you find yourself in front of another picket fence and gate with another sign.

You spend a minute or two studying this more complex maze. How do you find your way through?

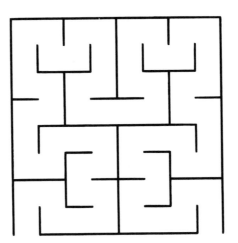

Fractal Maze 2 is a little trickier.

Eventually, you weave your way through Maze 2. As soon as you exit, you come to. . . . You guessed it!

Fractal Maze 3
Find the Way Out!

How do you find the way through this one? (Hint: Look for the fractal pattern!)

[Answer on p. 103.]

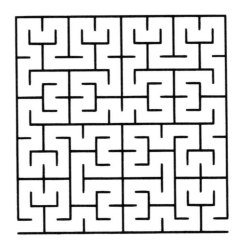

Fractal Maze 3 is quite a bit more complicated.

What a relief! When you emerge from the end of Maze 3, you don't find another, more intricate maze. Instead, you are standing before a stream that's about 10 feet wide. In front of the stream is a tree, with two loops of rope hanging from a large branch. Each loop is knotted at the bottom, and there's a sign on the tree.

TARZAN'S CROSSING
Swing on the knot,
not the unknot!

Which one of these two tangled loops is an unknot?

What fun it would be, you imagine, to swing across the river on one of the ropes, using the knot as a seat. But what if the knot were really an unknot, like the loops in Trek 1? Would it come untangled and send you sliding into the river?

Which rope has the real knot that will hold you?

[Answer on p. 104.]

The grassy path on the other side of the river leads to a miniature golf course.

Hole A is inside a rectangular wall behind a circular obstacle.

Hole B is inside an elliptical wall behind a triangular obstacle.

Hole C is inside a circular wall behind a rectangular obstacle.

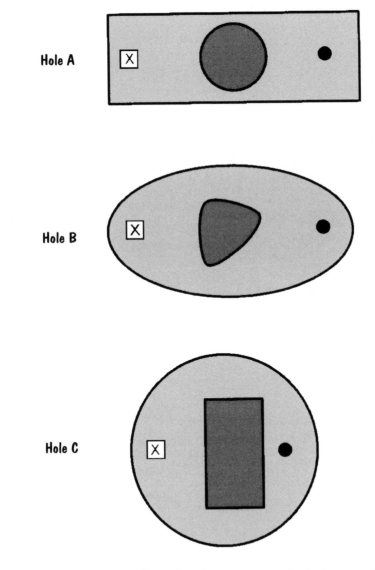

Hole A

Hole B

Hole C

Which is your best bet for getting a hole in one: A, B, or C?

[Answer on p. 104.]

As soon as you hit a hole in one, a bell rings, and a gate opens up behind the golf course. You walk through and come to a yellow brick wall. Peeking through a gap in the wall, you can see outside the MathZone to where you left your bicycle when you entered through the knotty gate.

The yellow brick wall has three gates, each with a different number. Below each of these base-ten numbers is a coded message in base two, like the message you decoded on the door of the Wild Game Hall in Trek 17. Can you find the right way out? (Hint: Look for the prime number.)

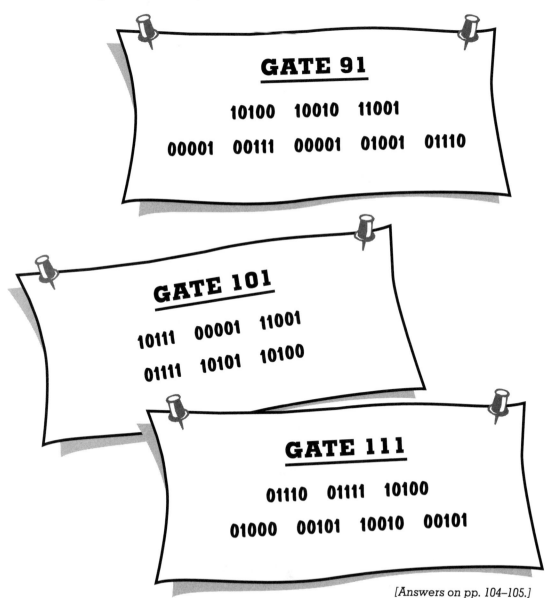

GATE 91

10100   10010   11001

00001   00111   00001   01001   01110

GATE 101

10111   00001   11001

01111   10101   10100

GATE 111

01110   01111   10100

01000   00101   10010   00101

[Answers on pp. 104–105.]

A Souvenir

"Here is your MathZone trophy," says a zany-looking droid standing behind the souvenir stand beyond the Way Out gate. You recognize the droid from the ticket window at the MathZone entrance.

"It's a Klein bottle," exclaims the droid, handing you a weird, twisty glass sculpture. "A Klein bottle is like a Möbius band with an extra dimension. It's a three-dimensional tube with an inside surface that loops back on itself to merge with the outside. How's that for a brain-full?"

"Awesome!" You take the Klein bottle, thank the droid, and head toward your bicycle.

Will your friends believe you when you tell them about the Math-Zone? Will they come back with you? Will it still be here when you return? Can math really be this much fun? Do the questions ever end?

"Come back soon," calls the droid, as you climb on your bike and speed away down the knotty path.

Answers..

Page 3.

Knot E is
the unknot.

Page 12.

The two states that force the use of a fourth color are Kentucky and Nevada, which are both surrounded by an odd number of states.

Page 13.

Here is an example of how a U.S. map can be colored so that only two states require a fourth color. In this case, the two states are California and Ohio (shown shaded).

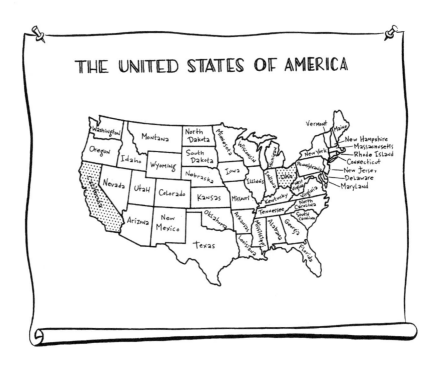

THE UNITED STATES OF AMERICA

Page 15. A map with intersecting straight lines as borders requires only two colors.

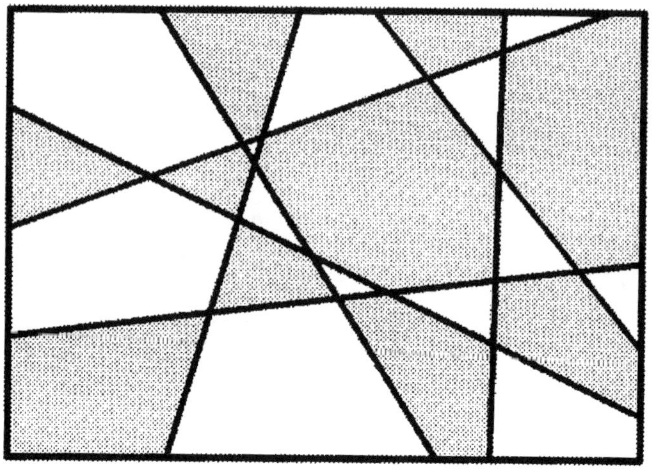

Page 29. All the Trek numbers are *primes*—numbers evenly divisible only by themselves and 1. Because 2 divides into 4, 4 isn't a prime number. The other even numbers (except 2) are also missing.

Page 31. Pick the curtain labeled with a prime number: 127.

Page 31. The numbers on the left, called *prime numbers,* are all evenly divisible only by themselves and 1. The numbers on the right, called *composite numbers,* are divisible by whole numbers besides 1 and themselves.

Page 33. The completed grid reveals the prime numbers 2, 3, 5, 7, 11, 13, 17, 19, 23, 29, 31, 37, 41, 43, 47, 53, 59, 61, 67, 71, 73, 79, 83, 89, and 97.

1	②	③	~~4~~	⑤	~~6~~	⑦	~~8~~	~~9~~	~~10~~
⑪	~~12~~	⑬	~~14~~	~~15~~	~~16~~	⑰	~~18~~	⑲	~~20~~
~~21~~	~~22~~	㉓	~~24~~	~~25~~	~~26~~	~~27~~	~~28~~	㉙	~~30~~
㉛	~~32~~	~~33~~	~~34~~	~~35~~	~~36~~	㊲	~~38~~	~~39~~	~~40~~
㊶	~~42~~	㊸	~~44~~	~~45~~	~~46~~	㊼	~~48~~	~~49~~	~~50~~
~~51~~	~~52~~	(53)	~~54~~	~~55~~	~~56~~	~~57~~	~~58~~	(59)	~~60~~
(61)	~~62~~	~~63~~	~~64~~	~~65~~	~~66~~	(67)	~~68~~	~~69~~	~~70~~
(71)	~~72~~	(73)	~~74~~	~~75~~	~~76~~	~~77~~	~~78~~	(79)	~~80~~
~~81~~	~~82~~	(83)	~~84~~	~~85~~	~~86~~	~~87~~	~~88~~	(89)	~~90~~
~~91~~	~~92~~	~~93~~	~~94~~	~~95~~	~~96~~	(97)	~~98~~	~~99~~	~~100~~

Page 34.   Choose either slide 211 or slide 223.

Page 49.   The fractal form on the top is called a Hilbert curve. Here are the first four steps for creating the curve.

Page 49.   The fractal form on the bottom is the Sierpinski triangle. Start with an equilateral triangle, then draw within its boundary an inverted triangle that is half the size of the original triangle (left). In the next step, draw inverted triangles within each of the smaller triangles created in the previous step (right).

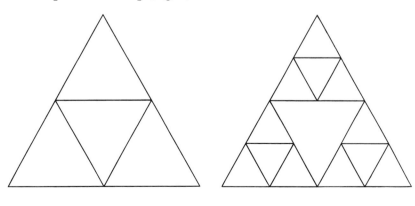

Page 51.	The perimeter of the Koch snowflake curve increases from 27 centimeters (original triangle) to 36 centimeters (six-pointed star shape) to 48 centimeters to 64 centimeters. At each step, the perimeter increases to 4/3 times the previous perimeter. The pattern suggests that after 10 steps the perimeter would grow to $4^9/3^9$ (about 133) times the original perimeter.
Page 57.	When you start a double pendulum swinging at small angles, it acts like a single pendulum, moving back and forth at a constant rate. Its motion is regular. When you start the double pendulum swinging at large angles, the two parts of the pendulum appear to move independently, and the overall motion, especially of the lower pendulum, becomes erratic and unpredictable.
Page 66.	Because there are more ways to get doubles and lose with the standard dice, you should choose the weird dice.
Page 67.	There are six ways to roll a double with a pair of standard dice and four ways to do so with a pair of weird dice.
Page 67.	Because doubles play a role in Monopoly, using the weird dice could change your strategy.

Page 74.

10100   1111   10101   11   1000

20 = T   15 = O   21 = U   3 = C   8 = H

10100   1000   101

20 = T   8 = H   5 = E

101   1100   1100   1001   10000   10011   101

5 = E   12 = L   12 = L   9 = I   16 = P   19 = S   5 = E

Page 76.   The first coded word is TOUCH.

Page 79.

Coded Message	11101010	11101111	11101001	00100101
Secret Key	10100010	10101010	10100101	01110101
Decoded Message	01001000	01000101	01001100	01010000

Page 84. The table shaped like an ellipse would give you the best chance of guaranteeing a hit.

Pages 92–93. The paths through the fractal mazes resemble Hilbert curves (see page 49).

Page 94. The true
knot is on
the left.

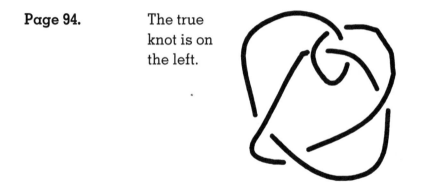

Page 95. Hole B. The surest way to get a hole in one is to try for the
hole with the elliptical wall. Because the ball's starting
point (X) and the hole are each at a focal point, hitting the
ball in any direction past the obstacle will make it
bounce off the wall and into the hole.

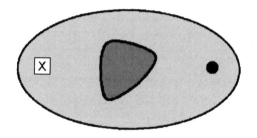

Page 96. GATE 91:

10100   10010   11001

20 = T   18 = R   25 = Y

00001   00111   00001   01001   01110

1 = A   7 = G   1 = A   9 = I   14 = N

TRY

AGAIN

GATE 101:

10111   00001   11001

23 = W   1 = A   25 = Y

01111   10101   10100

15 = O   21 = U   20 = T

WAY

OUT

GATE 111:

01110   01111   10100

14 = N   15 = O   20 = T

01000   00101   10010   00101

8 = H   5 = E   18 = R   5 = E

NOT

HERE

Glossary...

binary number A number represented in base two, using just the digits 0 and 1. For example, the normal, base-ten number 9 is expressed as the binary number 1001.

chaos A situation in which a system governed by simple rules or formulas appears to be random and unpredictable because tiny changes in starting conditions can lead to strikingly different results.

composite number A number that is the product of two or more whole numbers multiplied together.

ellipse A particular oval shape that can be obtained by stretching or squashing a circle.

focal point (focus) Inside an *ellipse*, one of two points positioned so that the total distance from one focal point to any point on the curve and back to the other focal point is always the same.

fractal A shape in which each part is made up of scaled-down versions of the whole shape.

Klein bottle A three-dimensional shape that has no edges and is twisted in such a way that is has only one surface. (In contrast, a sphere has two surfaces—the inside and the outside. A *Möbius band* has one surface and one edge.)

knot In mathematics, a one-dimensional curve that winds through space, with ends that join to form a closed loop, which cannot be unwound to form a circle.

Mandelbrot set A particular shape that is extremely complicated and has a boundary that looks like a *fractal*.

Mersenne number A number expressed as 2 multiplied by itself x times, minus 1: $2^x - 1$, where x must be a *prime number*.

Mersenne prime A *Mersenne number* that is itself a *prime number*. For example, the Mersenne number $2^3 - 1$ (or 7) is a prime number, but $2^{11} - 1$ (or 2,047) is not.

Möbius strip (or band) A continuous strip with one twist in it, so that the band has only one surface and one edge.

place value The position of a written digit as a factor in determining its numerical worth or meaning. In a *place-value* numbering system, the value of a digit depends on its position in the written numeral.

prime number A whole number that is evenly divisible only by itself and by one.

trefoil knot A mathematical *knot* with three crossings.

topology Sometimes described as rubber-sheet geometry, topology concerns the study of features that different shapes have in common even when some are bent, stretched, or otherwise distorted.

unknot In mathematics, a one-dimensional curve that winds through space, with ends that join to form a closed loop, which can be unwound to form a circle.

Further Readings...................

Visit the MathTrek Web site at http://home.att.net/ ~mathtrek/ to find additional material and references, amusing puzzles and features, links to websites on knots, fractals, maps, and other topics, and a chance to show off and discuss your own mathematical work. Send us e-mail at mathtrek@worldnet.att.net.

General

Barry Cipra. *What's Happening in the Mathematical Sciences*, 4 volumes. (Providence, RI: American Mathematical Society, 1993, 1994, 1996, 1998).

Keith Devlin. *Life by the Numbers*. (New York: Wiley, 1998).

Harry Henderson. *Modern Mathematicians*. (New York: Facts on File, 1996).

Ivars Peterson. *Islands of Truth: A Mathematical Mystery Cruise*. (New York: W. H. Freeman, 1990).

Ivars Peterson. *The Jungles of Randomness: A Mathematical Safari*. (New York: Wiley, 1998).

Ivars Peterson. *The Mathematical Tourist: New and Updated Snapshots of Modern Mathematics*. (New York: W. H. Freeman, 1998).

Charles Snape and Heather Scott. *Puzzles, Mazes and Numbers*. (Cambridge, England: Cambridge University Press, 1995).

Janice VanCleave. *Janice VanCleave's Geometry for Every Kid: Easy Activities That Make Learning Geometry Fun*. (New York: Wiley, 1994).

Trek 1

Geoffrey Budworth. *The Knot Book*. (New York: Sterling Publishing, 1985).

Kenneth S. Burton, Jr. *Knots: A Step-by-Step Guide to Tying Loops, Hitches, Bends, and Dozens of Other Useful Knots.* (Philadelphia: Running Press, 1998).

Martin Gardner. "The topology of knots." In *The Last Recreations: Hydras, Eggs, and Other Mathematical Mystifications.* (New York: Copernicus, 1997.)

Lee Neuwirth. "The theory of knots." *Scientific American* 240 (June, 1979): 110–124.

Trek 2

Kenneth Appel and Wolfgang Haken. "The solution of the four-color-map problem." *Scientific American* 237 (October, 1977): 108–121.

Lewis Carroll, with notes by Martin Gardner. *More Annotated Alice: Alice's Adventures in Wonderland and Through the Looking-Glass.* (New York: Random House, 1990).

Lewis Carroll. *Mathematical Recreations of Lewis Carroll: Pillow Problems and A Tangled Tale.* (New York: Dover, 1958).

Martin Gardner. "The four-color map theorem." In *Martin Gardner's New Mathematical Diversions from Scientific American.* (New York: Simon & Schuster, 1966).

Edward Wakeling, editor. *Rediscovered Lewis Carroll Puzzles.* (New York: Dover, 1995).

Trek 3

Stephen Barr. *Experiments in Topology.* (New York: Dover, 1989).

John Fauvel, Raymond Flood, and Robin Wilson, editors. *Möbius and His Band: Mathematics and Astronomy in Nineteenth-Century Germany.* (Oxford, England: Oxford University Press, 1993).

Trek 5

Martin Gardner. "The remarkable lore of the prime numbers." *Scientific American* 210 (March, 1964): 120–128.

Trek 7

Martin Gardner. "Mandelbrot's fractals." In *Penrose Tiles to Trapdoor Ciphers . . . and the Return of Dr. Matrix.* (Washington, DC: Mathematical Association of America, 1997).

Trek 11

James Gleick. *Chaos: The Making of a New Science.* (New York: Viking, 1987).

Richard L. Kautz and Bret M. Huggard. "Chaos at the amusement park: Dynamics of the Tilt-A-Whirl." *American Journal of Physics* 62 (January, 1994): 59–66.

Edward N. Lorenz. *The Essence of Chaos.* (Seattle: University of Washington Press, 1993).

Trek 13

Joseph Gallian. "Weird dice." *Math Horizons* (February, 1995): 30–31.

Martin Gardner. "Sicherman dice, the Kruskal count and other curiosities." In *Penrose Tiles to Trapdoor Ciphers . . . and the Return of Dr. Matrix.* (Washington, DC: Mathematical Association of America, 1997).

Darrell Huff and Irving Geis. *How to Take a Chance.* (New York: W. W. Norton, 1959).

Warren Weaver. *Lady Luck: The Theory of Probability.* (Garden City, NY: Doubleday, 1963).

Trek 17

Nancy Garden. *The Kids' Code and Cipher Book.* (Hamden, CT: Linnett Books, 1981).

Martin Gardner. "The binary system." In *Martin Gardner's New Mathematical Diversions from Scientific American.* (New York: Simon & Schuster, 1966).

Trek 19

Martin Gardner. "The ellipse." In *Martin Gardner's New Mathematical Diversions from Scientific American.* (New York: Simon & Schuster, 1966).

Martin Gardner. *The Universe in a Handkerchief: Lewis Carroll's Mathematical Recreations, Games, Puzzles, and Word Plays.* (New York: Copernicus, 1996).

Index ....